JACQUELINE
BOUVIER

Books by John H. Davis

THE BOUVIERS: PORTRAIT OF AN AMERICAN FAMILY (1969)

THE BOUVIERS: FROM WATERLOO TO THE KENNEDYS AND BEYOND (1993)
Revised and updated edition

VENICE: LIFE AND ART IN THE LAGOON CITY

THE GUGGENHEIMS: AN AMERICAN EPIC

THE KENNEDYS: DYNASTY AND DISASTER

MAFIA KINGFISH: CARLOS MARCELLO AND THE ASSASSINATION OF JOHN F. KENNEDY

MAFIA DYNASTY: THE RISE AND FALL OF THE GAMBINO CRIME FAMILY

THE KENNEDY CONTRACT: THE MAFIA PLOT TO KILL THE PRESIDENT

JACQUELINE BOUVIER

An Intimate Memoir

JOHN H. DAVIS

John Wiley & Sons, Inc.
New York • Chichester • Brisbane • Toronto • Singapore

Library of Congress Cataloging-in-Publication Data
Davis, John H.
    Jacqueline Bouvier : an intimate memoir / John Davis.
      p.   cm.
    Includes index.
    ISBN 0-471-12945-3 (cloth : alk. paper)
    1. Onassis, Jacqueline Kennedy, 1929- —Childhood and youth.
    2. Celebrities—United States—Biography. 3. Presidents' spouses—United States—Biography. I. Title.
CT275.O552D44 1996
973.922′092—dc20
   [B]   96-4332

Printed in the United States of America
10 9 8 7 6 5 4 3 2 1

To my mother,

Maude Bouvier Davis,

and to the memory of her late niece,

Jacqueline Bouvier Kennedy Onassis

1929 – 1994

The beauty of a race or family, the charm and benevolence of their whole demeanor, is earned by labor: like genius, it is the final result of the accumulatory labor of generations.

One must have made great sacrifices to good taste, one must for its sake have done many things, left many things undone.

One must have preferred beauty to advantage, habit, opinion, indolence.

FRIEDRICH NIETZSCHE

Contents

Preface xi
The Death of Jacqueline

Introduction 1
The Bouviers of New York and East Hampton

Chapter One 17
The Years of Bliss

Chapter Two 43
The Years of Dismay

Chapter Three 73
The Divorce

Chapter Four 79
The Remarriage

Chapter Five 91
A Divided Life

Chapter Six 107
The Death of Grampy Jack

Chapter Seven 119
Vassar and the Sorbonne

Contents

Chapter Eight   141
One Special Summer

Chapter Nine   157
The Inquiring Camera Girl

Chapter Ten   177
"The Wedding of the Year"

Acknowledgments   199

Photo Credits   201

Index   203

Preface
The Death of Jacqueline

The sudden illness and untimely death of Jacqueline at age sixty-four came as a bewildering surprise to me and other members of the Bouvier family. She had always been so healthy, so fit. As a young girl in East Hampton, she was physically strong beyond her years, with remarkable energy and stamina. She was also a fearless equestrienne who won her first blue ribbon at the age of five, riding a chestnut mare with her mother at the East Hampton Horse Show. I remember how she could outrace most boys her own age on the lawns of our grandfather's estate. The headmistress of her school, Miss Chapin's in New York, once told her: "I know you love horses and you yourself are very much a beautiful thoroughbred. You can run fast. You have staying power. You're well built and you have brains."

As she grew into her teens, Jacqueline developed a strong, muscular body and a poise and grace unusual for a girl in her so-called awkward years. I saw her more or less continuously during the first twenty summers of our lives and never recall her having a more serious indisposition than some pain in her lower back induced by riding her beloved horses so relentlessly.

After her burial at Arlington on May 23, I went back into my extensive files on the Bouvier and Kennedy families. I had written books about them in 1969 and 1984, and had not revisited those files since. There were hundreds of family photographs and papers, scores of letters dating from the Civil War to the mid 1950s, the wills of five generations of Bouviers, together with all the papers associated with the settlements of their estates, baptismal certificates, divorce proceedings, and all the volumes of my grandfather Bouvier's diaries in which he had faithfully made entries almost every day of his life since his marriage in 1890. My mother had inherited all these family papers from her father and had given them to me. Other documents, including letters and business papers, had come from my father's office files, for he had shared office space with Jacqueline's father for many years when they were both stockbrokers with seats on the Exchange.

I began sifting through this welter of letters and diaries and soon realized that they accurately illustrated Jacqueline's youth. These first twenty years helped form the salient qualities of her personality: her love of beauty, her strength of will, her somewhat cynical and mercenary attitude toward men, her need for more and more money, her physical prowess and stamina, her secretiveness, and her deep sense of history, which paradoxically, she did not apply to her own history.

Jacqueline was a remarkable woman in many ways, but she was a very private person. She revealed little of her personal life, her thoughts, or feelings in either her writings or conversations, and she remained somewhat of an enigma to her family, friends, and the general public all her life. She once made an offhand remark to a friend that might offer something of a clue to this aspect of her personality: "The trouble with me is that I am an outsider. And that's a very hard thing to be in American life."

Perhaps finding herself to be such an outsider led Jacqueline to conclude that whatever she would write or say about herself would either be misunderstood or considered impolitic. Perhaps, in the end, she preferred myth to history. A week after her husband's murder in Dallas, she gave her famous interview to journalist Theodore White at Hyannisport in which she vehemently urged White to characterize the Kennedy White House years as resembling the mythical kingdom of Camelot and not leave it to the historians, those "bitter old men," as she called them, to write its history.

"So the epitaph to the Kennedy administration became 'Camelot'," wrote White in his famous account of his interview with Jacqueline for *Life*, "a magic moment in American history when gallant men danced with beautiful women, when great deeds were done . . . and when the barbarians beyond the gates were held back. . . . Which, of course, is a misreading of history. The magic of 'Camelot' never existed."

This book is not myth, but it is as accurate a history of the childhood and teenage years of Jacqueline Bouvier as can be pieced together, written by a first cousin who shared those twenty years with her in New York and especially at our grandfather's East Hampton estate. It is an account based on both personal reminiscences and written sources available only to me of a woman who became, through extraordinary circumstances, arguably the most celebrated—or at least the most famous—woman in the world.

JACQUELINE
BOUVIER

Introduction

The Bouviers of New York and East Hampton

The family into which Jacqueline and I were born had been in America 114 years by the time of our birth. It had been founded by Michel Bouvier, a cabinetmaker from Provence and a foot soldier in Napoleon's army who had gone down to defeat in 1815 with the French emperor at Waterloo. Compelled to flee for his life from Royalist forces led by the restored Bourbon King Louis XVIII, he emigrated to America. He arrived, it is believed, with almost no money but with high hopes that he could establish himself quickly and profitably as a cabinetmaker in the New World. Family lore contends that this first American Bouvier had escaped from France "with a price on his head."

Michel Bouvier prospered in his adopted land. Settling in Philadelphia, he opened a shop, married twice (his first wife died young), and had twelve children—eight daughters and four sons.

Meanwhile, Napoleon's brother, Joseph Bonaparte, had arrived in America with a sizable portion of the Imperial Treasury and taken up residence at a magnificent estate on the Delaware, Point Breeze. Michel Bouvier soon established a relationship with Bonaparte, pointing out that he had fought with Napoleon, and went to work for him in various capacities, including making furniture for Point Breeze and building a small house for Joseph's daughter, Zenaïde.

By 1825, ten years after his arrival in America, Michel had so successfully established himself as a cabinetmaker that he was able to sell "twenty-four chairs and a conversation table" to the White House under President John Quincy Adams for $352. One hundred thirty-six years later his great-great-granddaughter, the First Lady of the United States, would sit on those chairs without knowing her ancestor had made them.

From crafting fine furniture, Michel branched out to importing Italian marble from Carrara and costly, exotic woods from Central and South America and began manufacturing veneers and marble tabletops. He invested his profits in real estate, including 800,000 acres of West Virginia coal and timber land, which he later sold at a profit of $100,000. He then built a huge, three-story palace in the Italian Renaissance style on Philadelphia's Broad Street with twenty-five rooms, including a chapel, adjoining greenhouses, and stables, and moved his large family into it on All Saints' Day in 1854. Michel had arrived.

After enduring the severe wounding of his son, Captain John Vernou Bouvier, at the Second Battle of Bull Run and at Gettysburg, Michel devoted himself to furthering the careers of his ten surviving children, one of whom became, with his consent, a nun. He married one daughter off to a son of the Drexels, a wealthy banking family. He gave enough money to two sons to buy seats on the New York Stock Exchange. Dying in 1874 at eighty-two, he left what in today's money would be a fortune of $10 million to his heirs.

One of his sons, Michel Charles, known as M. C., was to multiply his share of that fortune many times over and live in true Gilded Age splendor with three unmarried sisters in two contiguous New York City brownstones. Ten French servants looked after them, and a liveried coachman and footman drove them around the city in a maroon brougham. M. C., who donated a magnificent altar to St. Patrick's Cathedral in memory of his parents, did business with the financial titans of his day—the Vanderbilts, Drexels, and Rockefellers—and eventually became "Dean of Wall Street," an honorific traditionally accorded the eldest member of the New York Stock Exchange. He died, childless, in 1935, leaving the bulk of his large estate to his nephew, his deceased brother's son and the only male of the third generation, John Vernou Bouvier Jr. It was on his magnificent estate in East Hampton, Lasata, that his ten grandchildren, including Jacqueline and myself, spent every summer until his death in 1948.

Grandfather Bouvier was a gentleman of the old school who wore high, starched collars with jeweled stickpins in his ties, sported a waxed mustache, read the classics, and maintained a household where strict rules of dress and decorum were enforced.

John Vernou Bouvier Jr. had enjoyed a brilliant career in New York before inheriting M.C.'s millions. President and valedictorian of his class at Columbia, where he was elected a member of Phi Beta Kappa, he went on to graduate from Columbia Law School, becoming an outstanding trial lawyer who earned about $100,000 a year (that sum would be worth anywhere from $500,000 to $1 million today). A superpatriot who became General President of the General Society of the Sons of the Revolution and an expert on George Washington, he gave the principal address at the dedication of New York's George Washington Bridge in 1931, with such notables as New York Governor Franklin D. Roosevelt in attendance.

He also wrote a short history of his family, *Our Forebears,* in which he concocted an essentially fictitious genealogy that depicted his remote French ancestors as titled aristocrats who had served at the courts of the French kings.

On April 16, 1890, Grandfather Bouvier had married Maude Sergeant, the beautiful daughter of a prosperous wood-pulp merchant and paper manufacturer who had emigrated from Kent, England, as a child. He was twenty-four, she twenty-one. About a year later, the couple had a son, John Vernou Bouvier III. Darkly handsome, with a distinctly Mediterranean complexion and features, "Black Jack" Bouvier, as he later came to be called by his fellow stockbrokers, was destined to become the father of the future First Lady. Another son, William Sergeant Bouvier, known as Bud, was born two years later, followed by a daughter, Edith, in 1895. All three had the same dark, Mediterranean looks.

Jacqueline's grandfather, John Vernou Bouvier Jr., "The Major," with his twin daughters, Maude, on the left (the author's mother), and Michelle, right, in East Hampton.

Jacqueline's grandmother, Maude Sergeant Bouvier, standing on the red brick path of the Italian garden at Lasata, the Bouvier estate in East Hampton. Mrs. Bouvier, a lover of beauty all her life, won horticultural prizes every summer for her magnificent gardens.

So far as the John V. Bouvier Jrs. were concerned, their family was now complete. But ten years later Maude Bouvier became "accidentally" pregnant, suffered an attack of phlebitis as a result of her pregnancy that temporarily left her unable to walk, and on August 4, 1905, went into labor and produced two fair-skinned, redheaded twin daughters named Maude and Michelle. Maude, who was to become my mother, is now, at ninety, the oldest member of the Bouvier family, the last survivor of her generation.

John Vernou Bouvier Jr.'s oldest child, Jack Bouvier, was a charming and mischievous youth who was expelled from Phillips

The Bouvier twins, Maude (left) and Michelle, Jacqueline's twin redheaded aunts, at a costume party in East Hampton.

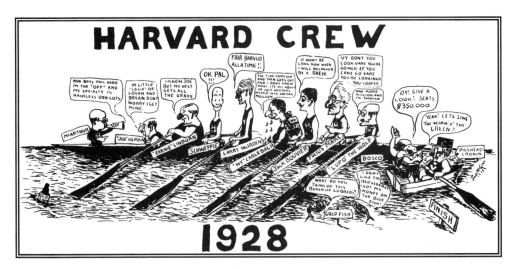

Cartoon depicting members of the New York Stock Exchange at the height of the Big Bull Market of 1928 shortly before John Vernou "Black Jack" Bouvier III's marriage to Janet Norton Lee. Jack Bouvier is the third oarsman from the right. One of Jack Bouvier's nicknames on the Exchange was "The Sheik," alluding to both his dark looks and his harem of beautiful young women. Jack Bouvier's marriage to Janet Lee took place in East Hampton on July 7, 1928. Their daughter Jacqueline was born on July 28, 1929. The stock market crash occurred on October 29, 1929.

Exeter Academy, attended two other prep schools, barely graduated from Yale, and soon became a notorious rake, playboy, and gambler, possessing none of the intellectual interests of his father. William "Bud" Bouvier also went to Yale, but he dropped out during his senior year to join the army. World War I was raging, and, as a member of a prominent French-American family, he was outraged by the German violation of French territory. He became a captain in the infantry, was sent to France with the 78th Lightning Division, fought in several major battles, and then was severely gassed in the battle of the Meuse Argonne and had to return home.

As for eldest daughter, Edith, known as Big Edie, she developed into a beautiful bohemian, an accomplished singer who probably could have had a musical career had her father not prevented her from developing her artistic talents. After marrying Phelan Beale, a lawyer from Alabama, producing two sons and a daughter, and then divorcing, she retired to her East Hampton home, Grey Gardens. There she became first a thrower of wild parties frequented by an assortment of poets, musicians, painters, dropouts, and oddballs, then, later, as she entered middle age, an eccentric recluse, living with her daughter, "Little Edie." She died almost destitute at eighty-two, after having been saved from eviction on orders from the Suffolk County Health Department in 1971 by her niece Jacqueline's second husband, Aristotle Onassis, who repaired the enormous hole in Grey Gardens' roof and installed a new furnace and plumbing system, enabling her to live out her last years in relative peace.

Meanwhile, the Bouvier twins blossomed into minor celebrities on the New York social scene. They were utterly beautiful, looked almost exactly alike, attracted scores of suitors, and became their parents' greatest joy. Both married in their early twenties, Michelle to Henry C. Scott, a star Yale football player and a member of the prestigious Skull and Bones secret society at Yale (whose members have included John J. McCloy and George W. Bush), Maude to John E. Davis, a Princeton graduate and a member of a Wall Street brokerage house founded by his father.

Every July and August, the family would all gather together in East Hampton at Grandfather Bouvier's fourteen-acre estate, Lasata (an American Indian word meaning "place of peace"), on Further Lane, which was then a narrow road running parallel to the nearby beach that faced the Atlantic. Beyond Lasata stretched acres and acres of potato fields; in those days, East Hampton was as much an agricultural community as a resort, producing an abundance of potatoes, lima beans, corn, and fish.

For the Bouvier grandchildren, Lasata was their own personal paradise. The sprawling seven-bedroom house, entirely covered with ivy, had a huge living room and dining room, and a glassed-in solarium that was the Bouvier grandchildren's favorite room, a place where games were played and mischievous plots hatched.

Albert Herter's portrait of the Bouvier twins, painted when they were twenty-one. The painting, which hung in the living room of Lasata, above the fireplace, was taken on a cross-country tour by the renowned portrait artist, who lived and worked in East Hampton in a house and studio overlooking Georgica Pond. The house is now owned by the industrialist magnate Ron Perelman.

The living room contained mostly heavy, dark, mid- to late nineteenth-century furniture, including several pieces made by the Founding Father, Michel Bouvier, cabinetmaker. Some of his tables held a gallery of Bouvier military portraits, including those of his son, John Vernou Bouvier Sr., in his Civil War uniform; his grandson, John Vernou Bouvier Jr., as a Major Judge Advocate; and his great-grandsons, John Vernou Bouvier III, as an Army Signal Corps officer, and William Sergeant "Bud" Bouvier, as a Captain in the Lightning Division.

Standing near two huge floor-to-ceiling French casement windows was a Steinway grand piano, the domain of Edith, who,

Mr. and Mrs. John Vernou Bouvier Jr. with their grandchildren at Lasata on a sunny August afternoon in East Hampton, 1935. Seated, left to right: *Henry C. "Scotty" Scott, Michelle Bouvier "Shella" Scott, John H. Davis, Jacqueline Bouvier.* Standing, left to right: *Edith Bouvier "Little Edie" Beale Jr., Michel Bouvier, Bouvier Beale, Phelan Beale. Lee Bouvier, Jacqueline's younger sister, is sitting on her grandmother's lap.*

whenever she got a chance, would fill the room with such songs and arias as "Indian Love Call," "Smoke Gets in Your Eyes," and "Un Bel Di Vedremo." Dominating the room was Albert Herter's magnificent portrait of the twins above the fireplace, a portrait that the artist had exhibited on a cross-country tour. There they were with their Titian hair and pale peach skin against a background of Herter blue, a shade of turquoise that the twins' mother had borrowed from the painting to decorate other areas of the room, notably the ceiling and window frames. Completing the room's

The nine Bouvier grandchildren on the lawn of Lasata, August 1935. Left to right: *Edith Bouvier "Little Edie" Beale, holding the baby, Lee Bouvier, Michel Bouvier, Phelan Beale, Bouvier Beale, Henry C. "Scotty" Scott, John H. Davis, Michelle Bouvier "Shella" Scott, Jacqueline Bouvier.*

decor was a floor-to-ceiling wall of books, and near a window overlooking the Italian garden were the backgammon and bridge tables.

The large dining room, whose prevailing color was the dull mustard yellow of its stucco walls, contained a long, heavy Jacobean oak refectory table, where the adults and the children over ten ate, and a smaller table near a window overlooking the front lawns, where the kiddies took their meals. Four large oil portraits commanded the yellow walls. On one wall hung a rather murky portrait of Michel Bouvier, painted late in his life after he had established his large family and his thriving business in the New World. A portrait of his wife, Louise Vernou, was next to his, looking down rather haughtily at the diners. On another wall hung Albert

Herter's stunning portrait of Edith wearing a diaphanous gown of Herter's trademark blue. Above the fireplace, opposite Michel and Louise, was a painting Grandfather Bouvier claimed was of the family benefactor, Joseph Bonaparte, resplendent in gold epaulettes and a sapphire blue uniform gleaming with medals. Later it was discovered to be a portrait of King Louis Phillipe that the king had given Michel Bouvier, by then a wealthy American, on his triumphal return visit to France with his daughters in 1853.

The grounds of Lasata, tended by two full-time gardeners and several part-time assistants, were spacious and highly manicured. The estate began not far from the Atlantic Ocean with a long post-and-rail weathered fence smothered with honeysuckle and swarming with bees whose humming could be heard from twenty-five feet away. The bluestone driveway led from Further

View of Lasata's living room with Albert Herter's portrait of Jacqueline's twin aunts, Maude and Michelle, over the fireplace. The doors to the left and right of the fireplace lead into the solarium. Some of the furniture was made by our great-great grandfather, the Founding Father, Michel Bouvier, who was a cabinetmaker before becoming a manufacturer and real estate investor.

Lane, curved through a vast green lawn under an arbor of young maples, passed by the main entrance of the house, skirted the four-car garage with the chauffeur's apartment above and the gardeners' shed, and eventually became a dusty dirt road running past a large cornfield to the stables and riding ring, where it finally ended in a back entrance on Middle Lane.

Behind the house a brick terrace overlooked a delightful Italian garden, Lasata's chief glory and the winner of many horticultural prizes. Here a neat geometrical pattern of box hedges and brick walks, similar to those found in renaissance villas around Florence, guarded the flower beds—blazing yellow zinnias, blue hydrangeas, orange tiger lilies—and led to the carved stone sundial. At the very end was a baroque fountain flanked by two statues of

The dazzling Italian garden of Lasata, the residence of Jacqueline Bouvier's grandparents on Further Lane, East Hampton, from 1925 to 1948. The ivy-clad, seven-bedroom house and red-brick terrace overlook the highly manicured formal garden, the winner of scores of horticultural prizes during the 1930s and 1940s.

View of the Italian garden at Lasata showing the red-brick terrace, the sundial, and the baroque statue of a French shepherdess.

French shepherdesses. A tangle of yellow roses wreathed the fountain, which was so mossy and weathered it looked as if it had been lifted from some Italian Renaissance prince's *giardino del piacere*.

To the left of the fountain, a moss-covered brick path led to the Grove of the Three Graces, where three nude attributes of Venus, sculpted from white marble, hands entwined above their heads, stood in a cool grove of fir trees. From there the path meandered to the red-clay tennis court, whose high backstops were matted with vines sprouting yellow trumpet flowers.

To the right of the fountain, the brick path curved past one of the French shepherdesses and a high hawthorn hedge to the "cutting" garden, with its annuals, sunflowers, lima beans, lettuce, parsley, and tomatoes, and orchards of peach, pear, and plum trees. Behind the orchards stretched the long grape arbor and the cornfields and finally the riding ring and stables, where on most summer days Jacqueline and her mother could be found either riding or grooming their horses.

Here from the age of five on, Jacqueline, in full riding habit—jodhpurs, boots, jacket, and whip—could be seen endlessly putting her mother's horses, a procession of "ladies' hunters," through their paces. I remember how determined an equestrienne Jacqueline became as she began thirsting after blue ribbons in the many East End horse shows she entered. None of the other Bouvier grandchildren, myself included, had that determination to succeed. We dabbled at golf and tennis and swimming; she really *worked* at her riding.

And so at Lasata the Bouviers lived their golden summers, glorying in a way of life few of them would ever again experience. The family had come a long way to reach their summer paradise in East Hampton. To live the life of beauty, grace, and luxury they led at Lasata in 1935, the year of M. C.'s death, had taken 120 years of struggles beginning with the plight of a poor French soldier in Napoleon's defeated army who had found himself at twenty-three with "a price on his head" and nowhere to flee but America.

Chapter One

The Years of Bliss

The summer of 1929 was a fruitful one for the Bouvier family—three babies in succession were born over a span of six weeks. I arrived on June 14, followed by Michelle Bouvier Scott on July 5, and Jacqueline Lee Bouvier on July 28. By mid-August of the most prosperous summer in American history, Lasata was teeming with young Bouviers. In descending order, Little Edie was twelve, Michel nine, Phelan nine, Bouvier Beale seven, and Henry C. Scott Jr., known as Scotty, two. Now they were joined for Sunday lunch on Lasata's mossy red-brick terrace by three squealing babies, to the utter delight of their grandparents, whom we called Grampy Jack and Marga Maude.

Jacqueline had been born to Janet Lee Bouvier six weeks late and weighed in at a robust eight pounds. She would soon develop into a captivating child with thick black hair, large, wide-apart brown eyes, high cheekbones, and a strong, muscular body.

Precisely three months after Jacqueline's birth, the great stock market crash of 1929 occurred, putting a temporary damper on the summer's euphoria. The Wall Street panic of October 24–29 was the second blow the Bouviers sustained that fall. On October 7, the John Vernou Bouvier Jrs. lost their younger son, thirty-six-year-old Bud Bouvier, to acute alcoholic poisoning. It was a

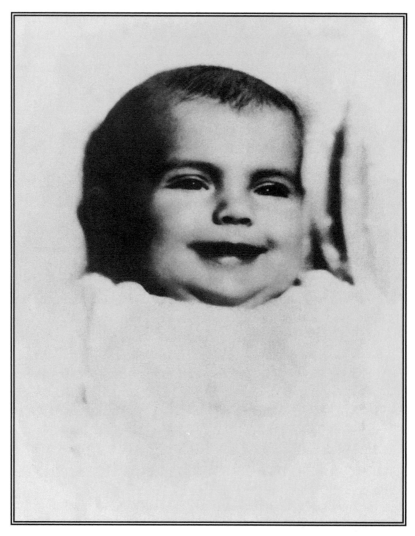

Jacqueline Bouvier as a baby. She was born in the Southampton Hospital on July 28, 1929.

tragedy from which Marga Bouvier never fully recovered. That calamity was, in turn, followed by the crash, which put a dent in the Bouviers' finances, but, thanks to M. C.'s astuteness, did not entirely wipe them out.

Fortunately for posterity, Grampy Bouvier, who was working for his uncle M. C. in 1929, kept a diary of practically every day of his adult life that presents a succinct and accurate account of the most devastating financial panic in the nation's history.

Sat., Oct. 19   Violent decline in prices.

Mon., Oct. 21   At office. Almost panic in prices.

Tues., Oct. 22   Recovery we expected came in early hours, then sold off.

On Wednesday, October 23, JVB Jr. made no entry in his diary. What took place was a six-million-share avalanche of liquidation, with the tape running 104 minutes late and an 18.74-point decline in the *New York Times* composite average.

Thurs., Oct. 24   *Black Thursday* ... Greatest decline in history of Exchange. Panic. No bids on some stocks such as ITT and PAK. 12,800,000 shares traded. All records broken. Called Jack.

Fri., Oct. 25   Market held. Steel opening at 207, closing at 204½.

Sat., Oct. 26   Slight advance. Sold 150 shares of C at 103½ ... Jack and Janet and little Michel with me in East Hampton.

Mon., Oct. 28   Market worse than Thursday. Steel down 17½ points. General Electric down 47½. Westinghouse down 34½.

Tues., Oct. 29   ***Blackest Panic Day of All* ... Record 16,410,000 shares traded. Enormous volume. No bids ... no bids ... Jack spent the night with me.

Although there were a few minor rallies in early November, and Jack Bouvier managed to make around $100,000 selling short, the general trend of the market continued to deteriorate. On November 6, JVB Jr. recorded the following entry.

> Market opened with a severe decline. Steel went to a new low at 166. Exchange closed at 1:00 P.M. Jack's $100,000 in profits swept away.

How did this catastrophe affect the Bouvier family? M.C. took it calmly. The veteran broker had experienced panics before—in 1873, in 1907, in 1917—and had not been financially injured by them to any significant extent. Although his assets had reached a peak in the roaring twenties of around $7,500,000, he emerged from the crash with $3,800,000. While mobs of enraged, impoverished investors were staging angry demonstrations in front of the Exchange and imprudent speculators were committing suicide in their offices, M.C. was serenely congratulating himself on his $1,600,000 cash reserve, his total lack of indebtedness, and the still intact value and quality of his municipal, corporate, and U.S. Liberty bonds.

As for Jack Bouvier, when 1930 rolled around and no improvement in the stock market materialized, he had to confront the bleak fact that his chances of becoming a rich man had received a near fatal blow. His severe losses on the stock market, combined with a sharp decrease in commission income from drastically reduced trading volume, made him vulnerable to a series of galling humiliations. He was compelled to seek financial help from his family, but was able to extract a loan of only $25,000 from M.C. and therefore was obliged to beg for aid from his father-in-law, James T. Lee, with whom he had never been on very good terms.

On December 22, the entire Bouvier family turned out for the christening of Jacqueline at the church of St. Ignatius Loyola in

New York. Little Michel, age ten, was godfather, taking the place of his recently deceased father Bud. After the ceremony, Jack and Janet held a reception in their rented apartment at 935 Park Avenue. Grampy Jack and Marga Maude, M.C. and his sister Mary, and Edith and the twins cooed over the five-month-old baby and gave Jack a moment of pride, in what had been a terribly demoralizing year, by telling him how much his baby girl resembled him.

On July 28, 1931, Jacqueline made her debut in the society columns as she celebrated her second birthday and attended a dog show in East Hampton with her mother and father. By then she was even more clearly a small replica of Jack, with the same wide-apart eyes, snub nose, dark hair, and olive complexion.

My earliest recollection of her was when we were about four or five. One summer afternoon Jacqueline burst into Lasata's bright, glass-enclosed solarium in her riding habit of brown jodhpurs, black boots, and beige shirt, covered with horsehairs, sweaty, disheveled, and reeking of her beloved horses. Michelle and I were very allergic to horses, and we immediately started sneezing. With itchy, swollen red eyes and runny noses, we both told Jackie to get out, go away, as we ran to the tissue box. "But she was *so great* today," I seem to recall her saying about her favorite chestnut mare. "We took all the fences so *clean!*"

Jacqueline was the first child of a rather unlikely, and, as it turned out, unstable marriage. Jack was thirty-seven, and his reputation as a ladies' man and rake was well established when he married the twenty-one-year-old high-strung friend of his twin sisters. Janet Lee was the petite yet athletic daughter of a nouveau-riche Irish family. An ambitious young woman, she was determined to marry a man who was in Society, and Jack Bouvier seemed to fit that bill. The Bouviers of New York and East Hampton had been in Society for several generations. Jack's great-uncle, M.C. Bouvier, whose wealth had made Lasata possible, had been listed in the first edition of the *Social Register* in 1887.

What arcane criteria qualified a man to be in Society with a capital S in 1928, the year of the Lee–Bouvier marriage? It is hard to pinpoint from the perspective of these altogether different

Jacqueline Bouvier at age three (top: with her mother, Janet). With her wide cheek-bones and wide-apart eyes, she is already beginning to look like a small edition of her father.

times, but I believe that in those days it was essentially a combination of four attributes. You had to come from a gentile family of European origins that had enjoyed wealth for at least three or four generations, had sent some of its sons to Ivy League colleges, and had at least one ancestor who fought in the American Revolutionary War. The Bouviers possessed all these qualifications. They had enjoyed wealth since the middle of the nineteenth century; they had gone to Columbia and Yale; and through John Vernou Bouvier Sr.'s marriage to Caroline Ewing, a member of a distinguished old Colonial Maryland family from Caroline County, they had a Revolutionary War ancestor who had fought as a Lieutenant with the Seventh Maryland Line.

Through her marriage to Jack Bouvier little Janet Lee achieved her ambition of entering Society. But it is likely she was not fully aware then that she also had married a playboy and gambler who had no interest in giving up his libertine ways. Jack Bouvier loved women, and he played the field both before and after marriage. I always thought that what he really wanted was a harem. Devastatingly and darkly handsome—in addition to "Black Jack" he was also called "The Sheik" and the "Black Orchid"—he would be stopped on the streets of New York by people who would ask for his autograph, thinking he was Clark Gable. As a stockbroker, Jack was more a riverboat gambler, and an in-and-out trader, than an investor. His fortunes rose and fell abruptly. One week he might be worth $3 million on paper; a month later, only a few hundred thousand dollars, or nothing. Jack Bouvier loved beautifully tailored clothes, sexy women, fast cars, and money. And it was probably for money that he married Janet Lee.

The Lees had emigrated from Ireland to New York during the potato famine at about the same time as the Kennedys, and Janet's remarkable father, James T. Lee, had enjoyed a rags-to-riches career very similar to Joseph P. Kennedy's.

Raised by poor Irish parents in a tough Irish neighborhood on Manhattan's Lower East Side, Lee was educated in public schools and at the City College of New York. After graduation, he worked his way through graduate school at Columbia, earning an M.A. and a law degree. As a young lawyer, he began working for real-estate developers and by 1908 had entered the field himself, building the twelve-story Peter Stuyvesant apartments in Manhattan at 98th Street and Riverside Drive. In 1910, he began work on what became an imposing apartment house at 998 Fifth Avenue that still remains one of New York's most luxurious and well-built residential structures. Designed by the prestigious firm of McKim, Mead, and White, the huge limestone building at 81st Street, with architectural elements of the high Florentine Renaissance, offered apartments of up to twenty-three rooms for such tenants as Theodore Roosevelt's Secretary of State, Elihu Root, and mining magnate Murry Guggenheim, who, with his six brothers, once controlled 75 percent of all the world's copper. In 1923, Lee went on to complete the huge Hotel Shelton (now the Marriott East Side Hotel) on 49th Street and Lexington Avenue, which, with its twenty-four stories, was then the tallest hotel in the world.

In 1928, the year of his daughter's marriage to Jack Bouvier, Lee, a man of many business talents, became a director of the Chase National Bank. The next year he began work on another luxurious apartment building, this one an ultramodern construction in sleek limestone, at 740 Park Avenue between 71st and 72nd Streets. In one of the apartments, a duplex, he allowed his daughter and son-in-law to live rent free from 1932 to 1938. This building, in the words of the *New York Times,* was designed to express "the new social power of Park Avenue." Lee went on to create more spectacular buildings while becoming first president, then chairman, of the New York Bank for Savings. Along the way he made a fortune, estimated by some to be in the neighborhood of $35 million.

Jack Bouvier was well aware of James T. Lee's financial success. Constitutionally averse to marriage, Jack would have considered marrying only if it promised him financial rewards. And, as we've seen, this marriage gave him those rewards.

Jack and Janet were also fortunate to be allowed to live rent free during the summer in East Hampton in a charming, spacious house owned by Jack's father. Situated on ten acres of lawns and potato fields, it was within walking distance of the Atlantic and a ten-minute drive from Lasata and was called Wildmoor, or the Appaquoque House. The Victorian-style clapboard-and-shingle residence was not nearly as large as Lasata, but it did contain six bedrooms and a widow's walk around the second floor where one could take the sun (which Jack did for hours on end) or admire the vast panorama of potato fields, salt marshes, cattails, sea, and sky.

By the time Janet married Jack Bouvier, she had already attained a toughness and a degree of physical courage unusual in a young woman of only twenty-one. She expressed her toughness in

Wildmoor, or the Little House, residence of Jacqueline Bouvier's grandparents on Appaquoque Road, East Hampton, from 1915 to 1925 before they moved into the bigger Lasata. Jacqueline lived here with her parents, Jack and Janet Bouvier, during her early youth in the 1930s. Jack Bouvier was suffering financially from the Depression at the time. Major Bouvier allowed him to live rent free at Wildmoor.

her quick and violent temper and a certain rudeness in her dealings with people; her physical courage was exhibited in the riding ring, where she demonstrated complete mastery of her mounts. Janet, who was my godmother, was a short, slight woman with sloping shoulders, a flat chest, and powerful, muscular legs. For an entire decade she was one of the East's finest horsewomen, consistently winning blue ribbons in every event she competed in, from the innumerable horse shows of the East End of Long Island to the National Horse Show in New York's Madison Square Garden.

As soon as her daughter could sit atop a pony without immediately falling off, Janet began training Jacqueline to become an equestrienne. Jack Bouvier, also a competent rider, assisted at these weekend training sessions in Lasata's riding ring. It was here in the adjoining stables that Janet and Jack kept their horses, which were looked after by the grooms, Willie and Murphy. My clearest memories of Jacqueline in her early years are of watching Aunt Janet trying to teach her how to ride a pony in Lasata's riding ring.

Jacqueline was around three when her training in horsemanship began in earnest. By the time she was five, she was able to make a good-sized horse respond to her commands and to participate in "family class" competitions in East End horse shows.

Mother and daughter riding their mounts side by side at these events made a charming impression. Here was the impeccably attired and unfailingly spunky Janet in her high black homburg, ascot tie, coat with contrasting collar and jodhpurs to match the collar, and tall leather boots, trotting alongside this miniature of herself, the confident little Jacqueline. I remember all the cousins sitting on the rails were in awe of Jacqueline's self-assurance on horseback.

Meanwhile, on March 3, 1933, Janet had given birth to another little girl, whom she and Jack named Caroline Lee Bouvier (Caroline was the name of Jack's beloved paternal grandmother). This child, who would turn out to be smaller, frailer, and prettier, in a conventional sense, than her older sister, would have to endure a life perpetually overshadowed by Jacqueline, even though she possessed her own considerable talents.

Four Bouvier cousins on horseback in East Hampton in 1933. Left to right: Jacqueline Bouvier, three, Henry C. "Scotty" Scott, five, Michelle Bouvier "Shella" Scott, three, John H. Davis, three. The adults are Jack Bouvier and his sister, Maude Bouvier Davis. Jacqueline was destined to become a champion equestrienne, whereas her other little cousins took no interest in riding.

Emphasizing Jacqueline's equestrian accomplishments does not do full justice to her other abilities and interests. An artistic child, highly sensitive to visual beauty, by the time she was eight, she was writing charming verse and drawing with crayon, pen, and ink extremely well. These abilities would come together in a whimsical book she and Lee wrote and illustrated in 1951 after a long summer trip through Europe that they titled *One Special Summer* and in which Jacqueline unconsciously revealed her concept of her destiny. In a montage entitled "Dreams of Glory," Jacqueline is depicted in a regal costume and a crown and is self-described as "Jacqueline, Fille Naturelle de Charlemagne."

1933 Mummy, Jackie and Lee 1933

Janet Bouvier with her new baby, Lee Bouvier, in 1933. The four-year-old Jacqueline looks on.

One of the most powerful influences on Jacqueline during her formative years was her paternal grandfather, Grampy Jack. Since she was the daughter and namesake of his eldest son, JVB Jr. had a special interest in and affection for Jacqueline as well as a justifiable pride in her achievements as a precocious equestrienne. When she went off to Miss Chapin's School in New York in 1935

Jacqueline Bouvier, age five, with her Scotty dog, near the garage of Wildmoor, East Hampton, August 1934.

The determined five-year-old equestrienne, Jacqueline Bouvier, looking annoyed as she leads her pony Buddy off the paddock at the Smithtown, Long Island, Riding Club after a rare horse show defeat.

and proceeded to earn straight A's in her courses and the special praise of the school's demanding headmistress, Miss Ethel String-fellow, his pride in her increased and he sent her congratulatory notes.

I believe that it was the influence of her grandparents and father, along with the environment of Lasata, that imbued Jacqueline

Mr. and Mrs. John V. Bouvier III and their daughter Jacqueline as they attended the Sixth Annual Horse Show of the Southampton Riding and Hunt Club on August 11, 1934.

Janet Bouvier and her daughter Jacqueline Bouvier at the East Hampton Horse Show in July 1935.

with her matchless sense of style as well as her taste in literature and the arts.

When Jacqueline was a girl of five, Grampy Jack took her to his Uncle M. C.'s brownstone on West 46th Street, where she was introduced to a world of Gilded Age splendor that left a profound impression. There she beheld for the first time the huge ceiling-to-floor gilt framed Louis XV mirrors in the red-carpeted foyer, the red velour portieres with golden tassels that separated the rooms, the paintings on the drawing room walls: two Corots, two Millets, a Rembrandt Peale, a Sully, and the portrait of Louis Phillipe as King of France that eventually found its way to Lasata's dining room. She saw the beautifully carved golden eagle, a gift to Michel Bouvier from Joseph Bonaparte, hanging from the red damask above the fireplace not far from the superb Tiffany chandelier at the room's center. She admired another Bonaparte gift, the magnificent white marble and bronze doré horloge (clock) with golden eagle and jet black sphinxes that Joseph had left Michel in his will. We can imagine how Jacqueline, with her acute sensitivity to visual beauty, was awestruck by all this magnificence.

Then there were those summers at Lasata, where she became immersed in a world of enchanted gardens, ancient statues and fountains, vast bright green lawns, great hawthorn hedges, and groves of miniature firs, delicate lindens, beach plum bushes, and stately elms.

And, finally, there was the example of Grampy Jack and Marga Maude, who observed a formality of dress more redolent of the nineteenth century than the mid-twentieth, and enforced it on their grandchildren. At Sunday luncheons at Lasata in mid-August the boys wore blue blazers, white linen trousers, shirts, and ties, and the little girls were attired in long-sleeved dresses with calf-length skirts, white knee-length stockings, and patent leather shoes.

I recall, in those pre-television days, how Grampy Jack would read aloud to us from Macaulay and Shakespeare in his book-lined study and encourage us to read only the greatest works of literature.

Jacqueline Bouvier, left, now six years old, and her sister, Lee, three, with their dog Regent at the Annual Dog Show in East Hampton, 1935.

In 1940, when Jacqueline and I turned ten, Grandfather self-published the remarkable Bouvier family history *Our Forebears*, which he dedicated "To my grandchildren and those who may later add to their joyous company." He inscribed my copy with a little poem:

> Jack, my lad, first con these pages
> And profit by your forebears' lives—
> While your interest still rages
> You may become extremely wise.

Our Forebears began with an epigraph from Lord Macaulay: "A people which takes no pride in the noble achievements of remote ancestors will never achieve anything to be remembered, with pride, by remote descendants." The book went on to recount the histories of the Bouvier and Vernou families in France, along with certain American families they became associated with through marriage in the New World. John Vernou Bouvier Jr. was fully aware that his grandfather Michel, the veteran of Napoleon's army who had emigrated to America after the Battle of Waterloo in 1815, had been a humble "menuisier ébéniste," a cabinetmaker, in the tiny Provencal village of Pont-Saint-Esprit, but he chose to ignore these humble origins and ennoble his grandfather. He used as his source an ancient volume of genealogy, which I now have, titled *The Armorial de Dauphiné* (Dauphiné was an ancient province of southeastern France). In the *Armorial,* the family of Bouvier is described as an "ancient house of Fontaine near Grenoble," a member of which was a "counsellor in Parliament" and was "ennobled in 1609." Grandfather took all this to be the remote history of *his* family and adopted the crest of these supposed ancestors—"d'azur au lion d'or; au chef de même chargé de trois huchets de gueules"— as his own.

But what Grandfather did to enhance the social status of his Bouvier ancestors was nothing compared to how he exalted his grandmother's French ancestors, the Vernous.

Grampy Jack hadn't the vaguest idea of where cabinetmaker Michel's wife Louise Vernou came from, but somewhere in his research he stumbled across a noble Vernou family in the Archives de la Noblesse et du College Heraldique de France, a genealogical society that once specialized in compiling pedigrees for noble French families, but was now defunct. This led him to declare:

> The family of Vernou is one of the most illustrious and ancient of the Province of Poitou ... it has been in existence since the year 1086 and has had many high honors and dignities conferred upon it. It contracted alliances with the

BOUVIER

The crest that Grandfather Bouvier adopted as his own. It belonged to the family of Bouvier described in an ancient volume of geneology as "an ancient house of Fontaine near Grenoble," which was ennobled in 1609.

most powerful families of the nobility of France, and was confirmed in its nobility of ancient extraction by two royal decrees of August 23, 1667 and May 19, 1719 respectively.

Arms: D'azur au croissant d'argent Couronne: de Marquis-Supports: deux Griffons—Devise—"Intacta Veneno." This device was given to de Vernou, Baron de Chancelee, Compte de Malzeard, Marquis de Bonneuil, by King Louis XIV, who nominated him a Chevalier of his Orders by reason of his resistance to Prince Marillac at the epoch of the internal troubles in France, wherein de Vernou by his example and his influence maintained the fidelity of the nobility of Poitou to the King.

Grandfather went on to list other noble de Vernou ancestors:

Bartholomey de Vernou, equerry, who in 1482 received his patents of nobility from King Louis XI, Louis de Vernou III, Seigneur de la Riviere and de Bonneuil who received in 1647 from King Louis XIV a letter urging his co-operation in the raising of men from the inhabitants of Poitou, and Marie César Antoine de Vernou, Baron of Bonneuil, Lieutenant of Cavalry of the Compte de Provence.

One can imagine how a ten-year-old child would react to reading about such an ancestry. Most Americans are aware they are the descendants of penniless, uneducated, working-class proletarians who emigrated to America to escape poverty or political oppression. But the Bouviers, and especially the Vernous, according to grandfather, had been members of the French aristocracy before coming to America; one of them had been knighted by no less a potentate than the Sun King, Louis XIV. This ancestry made the impressionable young Bouviers feel far different from most Americans, far more *special,* and I believe it gave all of us, especially Jacqueline, the illusion of a status far above that of the great mass of Americans and formed the basis of the aristocratic airs Jacqueline came to display as she got older.

Years later, in 1967, when I thoroughly researched our ancestry in France for my book *The Bouviers,* I discovered that both the Bouviers and the Vernous came from humble petite-bourgeoisie stock, that the founder of the family, Michel Bouvier, hailed from a family of carpenters and cabinetmakers, and that his wife Louise's father, John Vernou, had been listed in the *Philadelphia Directory* as a "hairdresser" and later as a "tobacconist." These discoveries did not endear me to contemporary Bouviers, who swallowed my revelations with considerable indigestion, and even caused some of them to turn against me. The point of all this is that the *fact* of one's ancestry can make no difference in one's self-image if one *believes* since the age of ten that one is a born aristocrat.

But I do not want to give the impression that Grandfather Bouvier was a charlatan who consciously gilded his family tree, knowing that what he was doing was issuing a false history to advance his social status in the eyes of his contemporaries and those of future generations. I think it was simply inconceivable to him that the residents of the palatial mansions of his grandfather, uncle, and aunts could have stemmed from anything but noble stock.

As a little boy, he had been brought to his grandfather Michel's twenty-five-room Philadelphia mansion in the high Florentine Renaissance style, with its private chapel, observation tower, greenhouses and stables, and garden filled with fountains and statues, and to his Aunt Emma Bouvier Drexel's vast summer estate in Torresdale, St. Michel, with its private chapel seating fifty and its vast barns and stables, and, last but not least, to his Uncle M. C.'s sumptuous New York brownstone with *its* private chapel, Napoleonic memorabilia, and ten French-speaking servants. *These* people came from the petite bourgeoisie of France? Impossible.

As it happened, what I discovered about Michel Bouvier turned out to make him a far more interesting and admirable person than he probably would have been had he been born into the French aristocracy. I learned that he had started out life in America as a combination carpenter and handyman. Records in Philadelphia's Stephan Girard Archives indicate that Bouvier was paid $10 by Girard for "repairing, polishing, and putting knobs on Secretary," $1.50 for "polishing diningroom table," and 50 cents for "taking down and putting up bed." As I have already pointed out, he eventually opened his own cabinetmaking shop and started turning out what are today regarded as valuable antiques. His great-great-granddaughter Jacqueline, eventually a bit disconcerted by my discovery in 1968 of her ancestor's plebeian origins, was immensely proud and pleased to receive two maple chairs in Empire style, made by Michel Bouvier in 1820, from a Pennsylvania donor when she was restoring the White House in 1962.

During the first six or seven years of her childhood in the late 1930s, Jacqueline led the life of a young princess, a happy, privileged interlude full of accomplishments among exquisitely beautiful and luxurious surroundings and doting parents and grandparents.

She also developed the tastes and preferences in people and activities that would last the rest of her life. Among her Bouvier cousins, she preferred the males over the females. She respected most our oldest male cousin and her godfather, Michel, who was ten years older, a powerful 6′1″ young man, nicknamed Big Boy, who could beat up any of us. He would thrill us all by tearing into Lasata's driveway at enormous speeds in Uncle Jack's black Mercury convertible, often with a glamorous young blonde at his side, stirring up a storm of dust and stones. At that stage in Jacqueline's life, I was too young for her. We were good friends, but since we were the same age, there was no particular reason why she should look up to me. Her favorite cousin was Michelle's son, Scotty, who was two years older, because he was so naughty and "bad." She admired his rudeness and his propensity to engage in such outrageous pranks as swinging down from the rafters of the Maidstone Club's ballroom at a Saturday Night dance, landing on a table, collapsing it, and spilling all the drinks on the revelers.

Jacqueline would continue to be attracted to "bad boys," rakes, older Russian emigré noblemen, and assorted scoundrels—a process that would eventually culminate in her marriage to the notorious international pirate Aristotle Onassis. As she once told a friend, one reason she was drawn to Jack Kennedy was that he was "dangerous, just like Black Jack."

But horses were her first and most enduring love. I remember going out to Lasata's stables on late summer afternoons and finding Jacqueline, after a day of relentless riding in the ring, in the stall

Of all her cousins, Jacqueline most respected Michel (left), shown here riding with his uncle Jack. Her oldest cousin and her godfather, he was nicknamed Big Boy, and he could beat up any of the other cousins.

Jacqueline's favorite photo of her father. Jacqueline, age six, is wearing the blue ribbon she just won at the East Hampton horse show as she holds Jack Bouvier's hand. Father and daughter were always delighted to be together. Jacqueline basked in the deep love her father had for her.

with one of her horses, grooming the animal with the most loving care, currying its mane and tail, hugging it, kissing it. I did not realize it at the time, but now I believe her obsession with horses stemmed from her desperately unhappy homelife.

Simmering beneath Jacqueline's outwardly charmed life was a mounting tension between her parents as Jack and Janet realized they had nothing in common but their two daughters. As early as 1935, when Jacqueline was six, life in the Bouvier household was regularly disrupted by shouting matches, temper tantrums, and mutual exasperation that frequently drove her to tears and desperate feelings of shame. By the age of seven, Jacqueline found herself facing the first major crisis of her life.

Chapter Two

The Years of Dismay

To behold the family of Mr. and Mrs. John Vernou Bouvier III in the summer of 1936 was to admire what appeared to be, on the surface, one of the most fortunate and attractive upper-class enclaves on Long Island. Jack, now forty-five but still handsome and in good physical shape, Janet, a slim, youthful twenty-eight, Jacqueline, a bright, captivating child of seven, pretty little four-year-old Lee, and the girls' strapping, athletic sixteen-year-old cousin Michel were spending the summer at Wildmoor, the spacious house on Appaquoque Road. Jack's maroon Stutz town car and Lincoln Zephyr stood gleaming on the bluestone driveway. Pedigreed dogs, chased by Michel and Jacqueline, bounded across the fenced-in lawns: Sister, the lively little white bull terrier, Caprice, the shaggy black Bouvier des Flandres, Tally-Ho, the temperamental Dalmatian, and the huge Harlequin Great Dane, King Phar, who was as tall as Jacqueline, and called "the best goddamn dog in the world" by Jack Bouvier. Residing in the stables at nearby Lasata were the Bouvier horses: Ghandi, Stepaside, Pas d'Or, Arnoldean, and the splendid Danseuse, who was destined to remain with the family for almost twenty years.

Not far away from Wildmoor was Georgica Beach, where diving into the surf was a favorite sport for the Bouviers, and,

Janet and Jack Bouvier shortly before they separated.

nearby, the mysterious Grey Gardens, owned by Jack's eccentric forty-one-year-old sister Big Edie, and inhabited by her glamorous nineteen-year-old daughter Little Edie, along with over forty cats. The large shingled house, once a showplace with its radiant hedge-enclosed garden, had become entirely overgrown with ivy and wisteria, its front lawn had degenerated into a field of wildflowers, daisies, black-eyed Susans, and Queen Anne's lace. Nevertheless, it was a favorite refuge for Jacqueline and her other Bouvier cousins because its atmosphere was so different from the formal, sometimes stuffy, atmosphere of Lasata. The children would stand enthralled around Big Edie's dusty grand piano and listen to her moving renditions of "Only Make Believe," "All the Things You Are," "Stardust," and Puccini's soaring "Vissi d'Arte."

A wedding portrait of Edith Bouvier Beale (1895–1977). In later life, Jacqueline's eccentric aunt, known as Big Edie, was rescued from eviction from her East Hampton house, Grey Gardens, which had gone to seed and was overrun by forty cats, by Jacqueline's second husband, Aristotle Onassis.

Big Edie was a great favorite with the young because, even though she was in her early forties, she was as irresponsible as we were, if not more—a wacky Auntie Mame who had no use for conventions and a hearty disrespect for respectability. Habitually siding with the children against their parents, she was distrusted by the Bouvier adults as a subversive influence to be barely endured at family festivals and ignored the rest of the year.

There were other realms in the Bouviers' East Hampton paradise. Grandfather Bouvier maintained family memberships in both the Maidstone Club—which boasted a Beach Club, a Golf Club, and a Tennis Club—and the Devon Yacht Club. The Bouviers owned a cabana at the Beach Club, as did Janet's family, the James T. Lees. There, in its three compartments, we all changed into our bathing suits before scrambling down the dunes to plunge into the roaring Atlantic surf. I remember Jacqueline, with her strong legs, most often winning the race to the water. One of the privileges we had at the Beach Club was that of signing Grampy Jack's initials to the lunch checks, as well as the checks for all snacks and drinks in the club's cafeteria. The Golf Club consisted of a large white-shingled clubhouse facing the ocean, an eighteen-hole championship course, and a tamer nine-hole course favored by Grandfather, who continued to play golf, often with granddaughter Jacqueline caddying, in his mid-seventies. Then there was the Tennis Club with its magnificent grass courts on which important amateur tournaments were held every summer in the days—late thirties to mid forties—of Alice Marble and Sarah Palfrey Fabyan and the great doubles team of Gardner Mulloy and Billy Talbert.

On the other side of the island, the Bouviers had full privileges at the Devon Yacht Club, which overlooked Gardiner's Bay, including, again, the opportunity to sign Grandfather Bouvier's initials for anything we ate, drank, or sailed. Devon was a club of such studied simplicity that it looked like a mere boathouse from which we could sail, swim, or fish for porgies off the club's long wooden dock that jutted out into the bay. One of our biggest treats at Devon was to sail out to Gardiner's Island, owned Robert Lion Gardiner, and in his family for over three centuries. Mr. Gardiner, whose first American ancestor, Lion Gardiner, had been deeded the island in 1639 by King Charles I of England, maintained a wildlife sanctuary on his domain where we would have the excitement of seeing rare ospreys and blue herons, white-tailed deer, and huge sea turtles.

Next to horses, Jacqueline's greatest passion was the sea. From an early age she loved going to East Hampton's Maidstone beach, where she delighted in the booming surf around her and the sight of seagulls diving for fish in the crashing waves. At the age of ten she began writing poems that were hymns to the sea. In one of these poems she confided that her most ardent wish was to live by the sea some day. Her wish was to be fulfilled four times in her life: at the Kennedy residences at Hyannisport, overlooking Nantucket Sound, and Palm Beach, overlooking the Atlantic; at her Aegean island home with Aristotle Onassis; and at her Martha's Vineyard residence during her last years. But all these sea places were tame substitutes for the bracing Atlantic beaches of East Hampton.

Despite living in a glorious setting and giving the outward appearance of being a happy, united family, the John V. Bouvier IIIs were suffering unbearable domestic tensions. I was an occasional witness to this discord, but the most knowledgeable and reliable witnesses were the maids and governesses in Jack and Janet's employ. Because of their testimony, given during the eventual divorce proceedings, we have some idea of what went on in the Bouvier household in the late 1930s.

After seven years of marriage, it was inevitable that Jack, the incurable Don Juan, would continue to stray from the marriage bed. While Janet remained in East Hampton all week, relentlessly training Jacqueline in horsemanship so that mother and daughter would never be outclassed by other women in their age groups— which, as it turned out, they never were—Jack would be in Manhattan, trading on the floor of the Stock Exchange all day and then heading uptown to relax at the Westbury Hotel's Polo Bar

A flirtatious Jack Bouvier holding hands with Miss Virginia Kernochan while his wife, Janet Bouvier, looks at the competitors at a Tuxedo Park horse show in 1934.

and Lounge. There, at cocktail hour, some of the most beautiful young women in the city would congregate and ultimately "the Black Prince" would succeed in luring one of these beauties up to the duplex at 740 Park Avenue. The woman would be so impressed by him and the luxury of the large apartment that it wouldn't be long before she would accept an invitation to spend the night. My father, with whom Jack shared office space on Wall Street, and who was more or less in the same position, weekending at Lasata and spending weekday nights at his New York apartment, used to tell me about the gorgeous women he would see accompanying Uncle Jack to restaurants and cocktail lounges on summer evenings. "Your uncle has a veritable harem in New York," he would tell me.

Word of Jack's philandering would inevitably filter back to Janet, and she would fly into uncontrollable rages when Jack returned to East Hampton on Friday evenings. This contrasted with the shouts of joy from Jacqueline and Lee as their father showed up at Wildmoor's front door: "Daddy! Daddy! We missed you so much. Let me tell you what King Phar did at one of Mummy's bridge parties. He knocked all the drinks off the butler's tray by just wagging his tail!"

Janet had been aware for some time of her daughters' preference for their father, and it further enraged her. She had a violent and uncontrollable temper. I saw her fly into one of her frequent rages one day at the Bouvier cabana at the Maidstone when she found a woman's bathing suit in the ladies' shower room that did not belong to her or one of her husband's sisters. I was the only other person in the cabana. "What is *this?*" she shrieked at me, holding the suit up between two fingers, as she let out a torrent of abuse against Uncle Jack that sent me fleeing into one of the dressing compartments as if *I* were the culprit.

Years later, during the divorce proceedings, Bertha Kimmerle, the Bouvier children's governess known as Mademoiselle, gave this sworn statement about Janet's temper:

> Mrs. Bouvier was a lady of quick temper which she showed many times toward Mr. Bouvier and which many times she showed toward the children. Indeed I had not been in their home more than ten days when Mrs. Bouvier gave Jacqueline a very severe spanking because the little girl had been too noisy at her play. She would spank Jacqueline quite frequently and became often irritated with the child, but for no reason that I was able to see.
>
> On Sunday, September twenty-sixth, Mrs. Bouvier called her father over to the house. I could gather that she was mad because Mr. Bouvier had not, while in town, gotten

himself a lawyer for some purpose. I do know when the three, that is, Mr. Bouvier, Mr. Lee, and Mrs. Bouvier, were together in a very noisy argument, little Jacqueline rushed up stairs to me and said: "Look what they are doing to my Daddy!" and at the time Jacqueline was in tears.

Janet was at a clear disadvantage in relation to Jack when it involved maintaining Jacqueline's loyalty and affection. Being with Daddy was an exciting adventure. He was always so debonair, he drove fast sports cars, and he bought expensive dogs and clothes for his girls. Saturday nights there would always be a dinner dance at the Devon Yacht Club and Jack would take Jacqueline and dance with his little daughter, much to her joy and the crowd's delight.

Janet was at a further disadvantage because of the tangled web of animosities between her parents, the James T. Lees, and Jack's parents, the John V. Bouvier Jrs. The family of tycoon James T. Lee, called Old Man Lee by Jack, was strange beyond belief. In 1903, Lee had married Margaret A. Merritt, the daughter of Irish immigrants, who bore him three daughters—Marion, Winifred, and Janet—after which he became totally estranged from Margaret, even though he continued to live with her for the rest of his life. Members of the Bouvier family vouch for the fact that, after Janet's birth, they never heard him speak to his wife again. It was as if she did not exist.

Complicating this curious marital situation was the strange position of Lee's Irish-born mother-in-law, Mrs. Merritt, who had such crude manners—and such a thick Irish brogue—that she was not allowed downstairs to meet guests for fear of embarrassing the family. Mrs. Merritt (who, of course, was Janet's Irish grandmother) was kept upstairs where she did all the knitting, sewing, and ironing in the household, functioning as a servant for all intents and purposes. During their courtship, when Jack Bouvier would go to the Lee house to call on Janet, he would always be dimly aware of an old woman sitting at the top of the stairs, straining to get a peek at him. When he would ask Janet who she was,

Janet would reply about her own grandmother, "Oh, she's just one of the maids."

To further complicate matters, Jack Bouvier's mother, Maude Sergeant Bouvier, never cared much for Lee or his estranged wife. Maude Bouvier was utterly devoted to her firstborn, and he to her, and she did not think the Lees were a suitable family for Jack to marry into. The refined Mrs. Bouvier found James T. Lee brusque and vulgar—he had no manners and was always chewing on a wet, unlighted cigar—and his wife an uncommunicative mystery. Although she couldn't help liking the spunky little Janet, she remained suspicious of her parents and never wholly approved of Jack's accepting the rent-free, luxurious Park Avenue apartment that Lee had allowed him, Janet, and the children to live in.

Relations between Jack and Janet Bouvier were no more loving at that apartment than they had been at Wildmoor. Jacqueline's governess, Bertha Newey, testified that Janet "was always tired and upset so that when you [Jack] arrived home from Wall Street, frazzled after a day of trading on the floor of the Exchange, she took it out on you." Bertha further testified that the Lees constantly interfered in the Bouvier household:

> JACK BOUVIER: Do you recall that after returning to New York after a very stormy summer on East Hampton, one day Mrs. Lee tried to slap Jacqueline in the face?
>
> NEWEY: Yes.
>
> BOUVIER: What did Jacqueline do to deserve such treatment?
>
> NEWEY: Positively nothing. Mrs. Lee, losing her temper, as she usually did, attempted to slap Jacqueline in the face, and I tried to shield her and received the blow myself, and then I very properly returned it to Mrs. Lee. A grandmother should never slap a child in the face and that's the reason I slapped her.

Admittedly, maids and nurses tend to side with a charming father over a cranky mother in marital disputes.

Another witness to the pain and tension of Jacqueline's family life in the mid-1930s was Bertha Kimmerle, who had also testified. She described Jacqueline as "an unusually bright and alert, but high-strung child, a little difficult to manage." As for her impressions of the Bouvier household, Miss Kimmerle further testified: "The air of the menage was not one of peace or happiness."

Despite her parents' bickering, Janet's temper tantrums, and Janet's bitter underdog rivalry with Jack for the attention and affection of her daughters, Jacqueline's innate emotional and physical strength at the young age of seven was sufficient not to let her unhappy homelife get the best of her. She continued to ride her horses far better than other girls her age, she did very well in her winter ballet lessons, and she was consistently an above-average student at school, far better than her father or future husband had been at her age. About the only indication that something was amiss was her extreme mischievousness and unmanageability at school.

At Miss Chapin's, a private and expensive day school in New York for children of wealthy and influential parents, the headmistress, Miss Ethel Stringfellow, was forced to scold and lecture the young Jacqueline more than any other girl in her class. Overcriticized and nagged at by her mother, overpraised and overindulged by her adoring father, and continually driven to tears by her parents' incessant quarrels, Jacqueline responded to Miss Stringfellow, who managed to calm her down and teach her how to persevere. Jacqueline would later tell a biographer that Miss Stringfellow had been "the first great moral influence" in her life.

Still, it came as a rude shock when, at the end of the summer of 1936, Jacqueline was told that her mother and father were going to separate. The separation agreement went into effect October 1, 1936, and stipulated that "the parties agree to live separate and apart from each other for the period of six months from the date of this agreement." It was further stipulated that

> Mrs. Bouvier, during the life of this agreement, shall have the custody of the children of said marriage and shall,

except as hereinafter provided, maintain, educate, clothe, and support said children until they shall have attained their majority out of payments hereinafter provided to be made by Mr. Bouvier. It is understood and agreed that Mr. Bouvier shall have the right to visit the children at all reasonable times and places and shall have the further right on Saturday afternoons and Sunday mornings to have them with him at his own home or elsewhere as he may wish.

In addition, the agreement provided that, for the six-month period, "Mr. Bouvier agrees to pay to Mrs. Bouvier on the 1st day of each month, commencing October 1, 1936, $1,065 for her support and maintenance and for the support and maintenance of said children."

This agreement was a severe blow to Jack both emotionally and financially. Emotionally, because he had to slink off to a single room in the Westbury Hotel while Janet and the children continued to live at the Park Avenue apartment. Financially, because he was now compelled to pay half of his after-tax income to Janet, leaving only $1,000 a month for him to subsist on. He had debts to his great-uncle M. C.'s estate and to the IRS totaling $64,000, on which he was obligated to make regular installment and interest payments.

The effect of all this on Jacqueline was to make her even more secretive. She had always been very reluctant to talk about her home life and the eccentric, ill-mannered Lees to her Bouvier cousins. We would often kid her about Uncle Jack and Aunt Janet's fights, which erupted at the Maidstone Club cabana, the riding ring at Lasata, and our occasional visits to Wildmoor. After the catastrophe of the separation agreement, Jacqueline became uncustomarily withdrawn. At Bouvier family gatherings during the winter of 1936–1937, Jacqueline's Bouvier aunts, uncles, and cousins began to sense an embarrassed, evasive air, as if she were ashamed of something. For example, when Jacqueline visited her Grandfather Bouvier's New York apartment at 765 Park Avenue and 72nd Street for Thanksgiving, Christmas, and Easter she went without Mummy. All her other cousins had their mothers with them, but she didn't. Of course, we all asked, "Where's Aunt Janet?" Lame excuses were made for her absence from the Thanksgiving and Christmas feasts, but, by Easter 1937, we all knew something had gone terribly wrong in Jacqueline's household. At those times she would nestle up to her father, as if to say "Well, I've still got him."

Janet, of course, would be furiously jealous when Jacqueline and Lee returned home and told her what a wonderful time they had had with Daddy at Grampy Jack's. In an attempt to weaken the Bouvier influence on her daughters, Janet went out of her way to involve them with the Lees. But Jacqueline never liked to visit her mother's family. For one thing, she couldn't comprehend why her Lee grandparents never spoke to each other, and she didn't like to hear Mrs. Lee make disparaging remarks, which she frequently did, about Jacqueline's Bouvier grandmother, whom Mrs. Lee detested and Jacqueline adored. And then there was always Janet's strange Irish grandmother lurking in the background, afraid to open her mouth.

The sixth-month separation agreement between Jack and Janet, which resulted in making all parties even more miserable than they had been before, ended on March 31, 1937. Shortly thereafter, Jack convinced Janet that, for the good of their daughters, they should try to live together again in East Hampton during the coming summer season. Eschewing Wildmoor because it had become associated with so many unhappy memories, Jack rented a much more modest house on the dunes not far from Lasata, and, as soon as Jacqueline got out of school, he took the family and the dogs to their new summer quarters in his maroon Stutz.

Although that summer would prove to be emotionally tempestuous, Jacqueline personally triumphed by winning the Southampton Horse Show in the class for children under nine. It was a magnificent victory at the East End's major show of the season, and it made everyone in the Bouvier family enormously proud. Even those of us, like Shella and myself, the allergic ones who didn't ride, conceded that the eight-year-old Jacqueline appeared

Jacqueline's oldest first cousin, Edith Bouvier Beale Jr., known as Little Edie. Little Edie was considered the family beauty. She never married, and now lives in Montreal.

in total command of her mounts and had become the star of the Bouvier grandchildren. She also upstaged the family's beauty, twenty-one-year-old Little Edie, known at the Maidstone Club, where she was one of the first girls to wear skintight latex bathing suits, as Body Beautiful, and the rugged eighteen-year-old Michel, called Big Boy, who would impress his younger cousins by driving fast cars and taking girls to the Devon Yacht Club dances on Saturday nights.

Jacqueline's occasional triumphs in the East End's horse shows were not enough to inspire an atmosphere of peace and love in the Bouviers' rented cottage, however. Again we have a document informing us what went on that summer. It is another sworn statement by Bertha Kimmerle, made on June 9, 1939, "in the matter of the matrimonial affairs of John V. Bouvier III and his wife, Janet Lee Bouvier."

> I had been in the home of Mr. and Mrs. Bouvier for barely a week when I could not help but notice that the relations between the two were strained and irritable. . . . This atmosphere in the household . . . consisted, among other things, in the lack of companionship on the part of Mr. and Mrs. Bouvier for each other. She was a lady that unmistakably had a will, and was generally engaged in doing what she wanted, when she wanted and where she wanted. It was thus a matter, of not daily at least of frequent occurrence, that Mrs. Bouvier was not home, and the children, consistently without their mother, were always in my company.
>
> On the other hand Mr. Bouvier was left in his own house quite alone, but his love for the children, and their very joyous love for him, I could easily see. Both were devoted to him, and both sought his company whenever it was possible. This was particularly so when Mrs. Bouvier, day after day, would leave him alone in the house. He seemed to get a real pleasure out of the children's companionship and it was equally clear that they got the same pleasure in romping, playing, and talking with and to him.
>
> This was particularly so in the case of Jacqueline, who, as I have said, was an unusually bright child, with a passionate fondness for horses. Little Lee was a lovable little mouse, not as high-strung or as alert as her sister, but strong, sweet, and affectionate.
>
> Whether it was lack of sympathy on the mother's part, or indifference, or because she was occupied with other thoughts, I do not pretend to say, but I did notice a certain reserve when the children were in the presence of their mother that they never showed when in the presence of their father.

In the end, the attempt at peaceful cohabitation failed during the summer of 1937. I dimly recall Jacqueline's unease at the ritual Sunday luncheons at Lasata. Despite her triumphs in the show ring, her mother's absence at these almost ceremonial affairs made Jacqueline uncomfortable. Inevitably, as we had at family holidays in the past year, we would taunt her with questions: "Hey, Jackie, where's Aunt Janet—doesn't she like us anymore?" To which Jackie, keeping her cool, would not reply.

The truth was that Janet had become fed up with practically everyone in the Bouvier family. Not only did she detest her husband Jack, but she hated Jack's mother, for Grandmother Bouvier naturally sided against her whenever a quarrel arose. Furthermore, she had little use for Grandfather Bouvier since he had given her the cold shoulder several times, and had stopped speaking to her father at the Maidstone Club. As for the anticonformist, irrepressible Big Edie, she had come to delight in making cutting remarks at Janet's expense, criticizing her for wearing short skirts after she had become "bowlegged" from too much horseback riding.

Janet, Jacqueline, Lee, and Bertha returned early to the apartment at 740 Park Avenue, while Jack repaired to the solace of Lasata to lick the many wounds Janet had inflicted throughout the summer.

In October, Jack attempted to live with Janet and the children once more in New York, but this trial reconciliation did not last very long and he was soon back in his hotel room with only the bar crowd in the Polo Lounge for company.

Bertha Kimmerle's sworn testimony tells us what happened next. Janet, determined now to divorce Jack, went out practically every evening, ostensibly prowling for male companionship. Bertha was left to take care of Jacqueline and Lee. As she later testified,

> Mrs. Bouvier left the apartment many weekends, leaving the children alone. This I would say occurred at least twice a month during the fall and winter of 1937 and 1938. I recall particularly that Mrs. Bouvier left them on New Year's Eve and was absent on New Year's Day, having gone

to Tuxedo with some man. It was at this time that Mr. Bouvier had already left 740 Park Avenue and when the children expressed a great eagerness to see their father, Mrs. Bouvier struck me as being jealous of the children's affections for him. I recall distinctly how this jealousy worked. Little Lee was crying for her father and Mrs. Bouvier said to me: "If Lee crys [*sic*] for her father spank her." The child still cried but I did no spanking.

I may truthfully say that Mrs. Bouvier had a very quick and at times violent temper, which she showed not only to Mr. Bouvier, but on many occasions when she was angry with me and with the children to whom she would frequently yell, and yell is the only correct word to use.

It is a tribute to Jacqueline that her turbulent family life did not prevent her from applying herself to her studies at Miss Chapin's—she continued to maintain her straight-A average. Still, the winter and spring of 1938 were an unsettling and often deeply unhappy time for Jacqueline and Lee.

During that winter, Janet devoted much more of her time to her burgeoning social life than to raising Jacqueline and Lee, who were eight and five, respectively. This responsibility was left largely to the evidently observant Bertha Kimmerle, who during the eventual divorce proceedings displayed almost total recall of what went on in Janet's household. If we are to believe Bertha, Janet was on a continual round of luncheons, bridge parties, cocktail parties, dinner parties, and late nights. The only fun the girls ever had was when Jack would occasionally sneak over and spend a couple of hours playing with them and the dogs.

According to the separation agreement, Jack had his girls all to himself on Saturday afternoons and Sunday mornings, including Sunday lunch. These became very special times for Jacqueline and Lee. On Saturday afternoons, Jack would take them shopping at F.A.O. Schwarz, Bloomingdale's, and Saks, and the girls would return home to show their presents to Bertha. Janet would inevitably be off on some weekend spree.

Sunday mornings were a particular delight. Jack would show up before the entrance to 740 Park in his convertible and signal his arrival with a special honk of the horn. The girls, primed for his coming, would run for the elevator, then race through the lobby shouting, "Daddy! Daddy! Daddy!" Jack would head for Durland's stables near Central Park where the three would spend several hours horseback riding along the cinder track surrounding the reservoir. Then he would take them back to the Westbury for club sandwiches in the Polo Bar, where he would enjoy the admiring glances the patrons and waiters would give his charming little girls.

When Janet returned from her weekend jaunts, her life was made unintentionally miserable by her girls telling her what a *wonderful* time they had had with Daddy. Janet was repeatedly driven to distraction by her daughters' love for their father, so much so that when June finally rolled around she told Jack that she and the girls were *not* going to share a house with him for the summer. They would rent their own place at Bellport, a small, unfashionable village to the west of East Hampton, not far from Southampton, and he could stay at the cottage on the dunes by himself. And that was that.

There followed a repeat of the winter routine. Janet spent most of her time away from the house, frequently visiting her parents and attending cocktail parties to which she made sure in advance Jack was not invited. As for Jacqueline, she was at Lasata's stables and riding ring, endlessly putting the horses through their paces and waiting, waiting for Daddy to arrive for the weekend.

Bernice Anderson, a maid in Janet's Bellport household, had this to say at the divorce proceedings:

> The children, with the atmosphere the way it was and their mother highly nervous and irritable, were not happy at Bellport, and Jacqueline frequently spoke about running away and going to her father's house at East Hampton. Once, when her mother was away, Jacqueline asked me to help her find her father's number in the telephone book as she was so unhappy she wanted to talk to him without

delay. In fact, I never saw two happier children than the day Mr. Bouvier called for them at Bellport.

To Jacqueline's and Lee's joy, Jack decided to take the whole month of August 1938 off so he could be with his girls as much as possible. On July 28, Jacqueline celebrated her ninth birthday. She was fawned over by her adoring relatives at Lasata, but Janet was not present. Jacqueline was now a striking young girl with thick black hair, which she often wore in a long pigtail down her back, a lean body, and long, muscular legs with well-defined calves. To the outside world, she was a champion equestrienne, a mischievous tomboy, and an A student at school, but the relentless tension between her parents made her acutely unhappy and often secretive with those close to her.

Her birthday was celebrated in Lasata's large dining room, with everyone seated at the long oaken refectory table covered with an aging beige lace tablecloth. A typical Bouvier birthday lunch would start with either tomatoes stuffed with crabmeat or jellied madrilene, and proceed to roast Long Island duckling with stuffing and applesauce, Lasata baby limas, and corn on the cob. At birthday feasts, practically everything on the table had been grown at Lasata. The birthday cake would be served with home-made peach ice cream churned by Adam, the chauffeur, that was topped with chocolate sauce; the birthday song would be chiefly sung by Big Edie, whose powerful soprano voice drowned out all others.

During the meal, conversation would be desultory and some-times argumentative. Jack Bouvier had the habit of complimenting his children to their faces and defending them against what he would interpret as slights from the other grandchildren. "Doesn't Jackie look terrific?," he would say, glancing at his father at the head of the table and his sisters. "Girl's taken all prizes in her class so far this summer, the whole lot of them . . . and she's always the prettiest thing in the ring to boot." Or "Jackie's got every boy of the Maidstone after her and the kid's not even ten . . . what are we going to do with her when she's twenty?"

Jacqueline's adult relatives were accustomed to these tributes and did not rise to them. Grandfather, if he had his hearing aid turned on, would acknowledge their appropriateness with a nod of the head and a smile. They were not received with enthusiasm by the other grandchildren, however, and usually provoked jibes at her expense. Uncle Jack would smile at his nieces' and nephews' protests and then would make them even more envious by flattering his younger daughter, Lee. "Lee's going to be a real glamor girl some day. . . . Will you look at those eyes . . . and those sexy lips of hers?" That Jackie and Lee thrived on these compliments was obvious: when the whole family was present, they received continuous transfusions of self-esteem from him. No wonder they preferred his company to that of their often carping mother.

But birthday lunches at Lasata were not always peaceful. From one minute to the next there could be an eruption of minor violence. Snap! A miniature explosion, followed by a scream, would suddenly distract everyone from Jack's flattery. Michelle's son, Scotty, had just exploded a snapper in Jackie's face. There were no burns, no wounds, only shock and outrage. Jackie soon had her emotions under control, but her father was slower to cool. Jack defended his children as vigorously as he complimented them. Turning on his guilty nephew, he let loose a barrage of abuse that left the rugged little boy paralyzed with dismay. The snapper could have blinded Jackie for life, ruined her beauty, put an end to her riding career, curtailed her schooling, killed her . . . from blood poisoning. Heedless of those who came to Scotty's defense, Jack went on to remind Maudie that *her* son was just as guilty; *he* had thrown sand in Jackie's face at the beach three days ago. *That* could have put her eyes out *too.* By God, if there was any more of this molesting of his daughter, he would put an end to it, all right—he would break the offender's neck or call a cop and have the kid brought to juvenile court!

It took a while for Black Jack to subside. With menacing gestures toward Michelle and Scotty, he informed her how badly she had brought her son up, how undisciplined he and all the other grandchildren were, and how nobody appreciated Jackie's talents, otherwise they wouldn't throw sand at her or explode snappers in her face. "*What* talents?" demanded an unwary grandchild, implying by her tone of voice that there were none. "Her *riding,* among others," retorted Jack, "she's only won *all* the first prizes this year—where have *you* been?" And the grandchild would reply, "Oh, *anybody* can ride. . . ."

Although the initial outburst aroused Grandfather, he soon lapsed back into his exclusive interest in his own occupations. Turning his hearing aid down, he muttered something to the effect that if Jackie married a jockey, the molestation would be worse, then took to trying out new golf grips with his dessert spoon. Suddenly the mood of contention would be dissipated by the arrival of the birthday cake and Edith's chandelier-rattling voice as she launched into the birthday song with the gusto of an opera star belting out the first bars of a Verdi aria.

After the birthday lunch, everyone would spill out onto the brick terrace overlooking the Italian garden for demitasse and candies. Then Jackie would change into her riding habit and race out to the paddock to put Danseuse, whom Willie had already saddled up, through her paces, while her other cousins would head for the beach.

August 1938 turned out to be a joyful month for the entire Bouvier family. Jack had his girls with him practically every day. Jacqueline won another blue ribbon at the East Hampton Horse Show. The whole family turned up at Lasata on August 4 for my mother's and her twin sister's birthday, and a huge family reunion took place on August 12 to celebrate Grandfather Bouvier's seventy-third birthday, at which Jacqueline read a poem she had written in praise of Grampy Jack. Lasata never looked more glorious. Unusually heavy spring rains had made the estate's great lawns even greener, and the sunken, hedge-enclosed Italian garden with its zinnias, marigolds, and dahlias was ablaze in orange and gold.

The heavy rains had also brought forth an unusually large harvest of peaches, plums, grapes, corn, tomatoes, and lima beans.

As usual, Big Edie led the birthday song; then, after Adam's ice cream and the blowing out of the candles on the cake, the grandchildren raced out of the house to play with Caprice and the gigantic King Phar, and, of course, Jacqueline tore back to the stables and the riding ring. Soon she would be taking Danseuse over the fences.

Yes, life was wonderful at Lasata during that radiant summer of 1938. Among other excitements, Jack introduced an exotic new friend to his girls, Baron George de Mohrenschildt, a White Russian émigré who worked on Wall Street and came out to the Island on weekends. He took a shine to Jack's younger sister, Michelle, and was soon hanging around Lasata all the time.

The Baron expressed a special interest in Jacqueline and her talents as an equestrienne. An able horseman himself, the tall, physically robust de Mohrenshildt had learned to ride on the family estate in Russia. He used to say that Lasata reminded him of that estate, which had been confiscated by the Bolsheviks. For about five weeks that summer, Jack, George, Jacqueline, Lee, and Michelle were always doing things together; Jacqueline conceived such a liking for the dashing nobleman that she called him Uncle George. After the collapse of Jack and Janet's marriage, and the dissolution of his romance with Michelle, de Mohrenschildt ended up in Texas, where, by a curious set of circumstances, he became the principal mentor and friend of a young man named Lee Harvey Oswald, the husband of another Russian émigré, Marina Prusakova.

Jacqueline's and Lee's governess testified in divorce court about Jack Bouvier's behavior with his girls during that charmed summer. According to Bertha Kimmerle, Mr. Bouvier

> was during this holiday the most careful of fathers, particularly regarding the children's routine day as to their hours of play, a time for rest, a time for their meals, their going

to bed, and their swimming exercises in the morning at
the beach, and Jacqueline's riding in the afternoon . . . and
it is a fact that they were very sorry weeping little girls
when Mr. Bouvier's custody came to an end, and they
were compelled to return to their mother who was staying
with her father, Mr. Lee, in East Hampton.

The restless Janet had, by mid-August, given up her experi-
ment with the Bellport cottage and had moved in with her father
in East Hampton for the duration of the summer. Bertha Kimmerle
accompanied Janet and described what life was like at Mr. Lee's:

> The experience with Mr. Lee, so far as food and routine
> was concerned, was exactly the opposite as that they had
> gone through at Mr. Bouvier's. There was really no estab-
> lished hours for meals, and the children would be served
> with canned foods, canned soup, and canned fruit, as in
> comparison with the fresh vegetables, fruits, and soups
> they received at their father's home.

At summer's end, Mr. Lee, a forceful man who detested Jack
Bouvier and had little use for the other Bouviers, decided to take
his daughter's marital troubles into his own hands. First, he forced
Janet to give up the duplex in his building at 740 Park, insisting
that it was much too large for a family of three. He settled them
into a smaller rental flat at 1 Gracie Square, an attractive and fashionable residential area not far from Miss Chapin's School and
Gracie Mansion, Mayor Fiorello LaGuardia's official residence.
Janet's maid, Bernice Anderson, testified about Janet's unhappy life
in her new apartment:

> I was at 1 Gracie Square with Mrs. Bouvier and the chil-
> dren from October 1, 1938, until two or three days before
> Thanksgiving Day of the same year. Here things were
> about as they were at Bellport, if not worse. Mrs. Bouvier
> always stayed in bed until 12 o'clock, getting up only in

time for lunch. Mrs. Bouvier was highly nervous all during this time that I was with her at this address, and drank even more than at Bellport and almost every night she used to take sleeping pills (Allonal) to put her to sleep. . . . Mr. Lee was a constant dinner guest, at least once a week; they would talk late into the night.

We can imagine what Janet and her father would discuss "late into the night." Old Man Lee hated Jack Bouvier almost as much as Janet did and was just as anxious to get rid of him. According to Bernice Anderson's final testimony, family life at 1 Gracie Square was going from bad to worse:

Jacqueline used to say on many occasions that she hated her mother. Jacqueline and her mother frequently had yelling spells; she would yell at Jacqueline and Jacqueline would yell back at her mother. In fact they both were very high-strung and Mrs. Bouvier seemed to be by far the worse of the two. In closing I would say that the children were not happy with their mother at Bellport or at Gracie Square. They always seemed very happy when they were allowed by their mother to go see their father, in fact it was almost pathetic.

It was a desperately unhappy situation for all concerned. For Jack Bouvier, his daughters were his life. They alone gave his life meaning and made the daily grind on Wall Street worthwhile. And, for Jacqueline and Lee, their father was the center of their existence, the person they loved more than anyone else in the world.

For Janet, Jack Bouvier stood between her and her daughters as well as in the way of a new life. If she could divorce Jack Bouvier, and remarry, she could then take the children away from their father once and for all. Jack, of course, was not about to grant Janet a divorce, because upon a possible remarriage Janet could make it extremely difficult for him to see his beloved daughters.

From a legal standpoint, the only grounds for absolute divorce in New York at that time was adultery. If you could conclusively prove adultery in court, you did not need the other partner's consent to obtain a legal divorce. And so Janet and her father concocted what they thought was an ingenious plot to trap Jack in an adulterous situation. They hired detectives to keep Jack Bouvier under observation night and day. They even hired a certain "Scandinavian blonde" to entice him into bed. After a while, Janet and Old Man Lee believed they had their evidence. But did they?

Jack Bouvier's father left an account of this adventure written in his inimitable florid prose. It was inherited by my mother along with all his other papers. Mr. X is Janet's father, James T. Lee.

HIST! HIST!

OR

THE TERRIBLE "TEC"

Listen my children and then you shall hear
The funniest story of all the long year,
Of snipers and snoopers and gum-shoe sleuths,
Conducting their hunt from telephone booths.
With peroxide blondes engaged in the race,
And 'partment house servants joining the chase.

Mr. "X" is or was, or hopes to be, a Napoleon of finance. Having acquired the taste of money-power by some parlous shrewd real-estate ventures which at the outset netted him unusually tidy returns, it was not long before he recognized himself to be, in this particular field, an expert, while later he was accepted by some of the less discerning of the community at his own high evaluation. . . .

Now Mr. "X" in his halcyon and ebullient days had several daughters, all of whom are married, but his own marital sun has been in complete eclipse for over a fifth of a century, which fact probably gave him ideas. At all events, one of his three graces wed a respectable young man with a reasonably sound background that did not partake of the sandlots, supplemented by an education that a University is sometimes enabled to provide. Of this union there were, happily, born several children, running, however, to an identical sex, which rather missed an agreeable nursery variety that tends to add spice to a menage.

Passed then the years, and with them some of the glamour of matrimony; rather stressed by the wife, as in age she was not inconsiderably younger than her spouse. Viewpoints are rather prone to be dissimilar when eyes are not severally adjusted to the same horizons. At all events, there appeared to arise certain differences, not necessarily fundamental, but nevertheless, calculated to dull the edge of mutual enthusiasm. . . .

Skipping lightly, as do historical compendiums over centuries of Civilization's Progress, there came a time when Mr. "X," not unlike Napoleon, who claimed to be his own ancestor, concluded he could encompass bricks, banks, and benedicts. Then a new star floated in the firmament, Mr. "X" became pregnant with an idea and parturition was in the vestibule of events.

Called him about him, his satellites, minions hirelings, detectives, male and female, his employees and casual comrades. Deeply did he meditate and warily did he plan. A divorce inexorable, from bed, board and the kitchenette was definitely indicated, but how to proceed, how best to trip, trap, tie and torture his victim.

Obviously there had to be a woman, factitious, fictitious, fortuitous and feminine, in order to meet the ethical and legal requirements of the Empire State concerned with absolute divorce. . . .

An abiogenetic thought then burgeoned, beautiful and bewildering; he would be a Pygmalion,* fashioning his

---

*In Greek mythology, Pygmalion, a gifted young sculptor from Cyprus, was a woman hater. However, he labored long and devotedly on a statue of a young woman, whom he called Galatea, and with whom he fell in love. He prayed to the goddess of love, Aphrodite, to bring the statue to life. She answered his prayer. The statue came to life and Pygmalion conceived a passionate sexual attraction for her, married her, and had a son from her, Paphos, who gave his name to Aphrodite's favorite city.

---

own Galatea and not invoke Aphrodite, but his discerning detectives and secretive sleuths to give her life.

Promptly our Colossus of contraptions marshalled his forces: Three detectives, his apartment house superintendent, doormen and elevator operators of his remaining real-estate adventures, which had maintained some of its financial integrity. The superintendent was to be the liaison officer between the Intelligence Department and the Paymaster-General. Incidentally, he could, with doormen and elevator operators, provide the requisite legal corroboration. To lend color, eclat, and a touch of the Byzantine, a woman was to be introduced as one of the dramatis personae.

The plot was ingenious, the action thrilling, the denouement mystifying, but the actors were hams. Across the street from where lived the victim, two snappy sleuths, readily identifiable for exactly what they were, kept watch and ward. That the "props" might lack nothing of verisimilitude, they rented the ground floor. Each night any casual pedestrian could observe their leveled field glasses and overhear their hopeful exchanges.

The better to conceal their identities, they looked like detectives, dressed like detectives, and acted like detectives. There was but one trifling omission, they failed to detect. But this to them was of course negligible. With a wage of ten dollars per diem plus expenses while engaged in the congenial quest of finding something or somebody, why exhaust the economic potentialities by finding either a person or a thing, as long as one is paid for searching. . . .

Between the home of Galatea to the apartment of her putative lover they wandered at early morn, midday and vesper-tide, with binoculars conveniently accessible for distant views of fading perspectives. Ye gods! how they watched and at what pains they were to let the whole world know who and what they were watching. Their perseverance was sublime, their ingenuousness bucolicly beautiful, and their purposiveness dutifully undeflected. But no Galatea and no informal companion to report.

They, however, were only the outposts before the walls of Troy. The Wooden Horse, not as a gift, but as a guest, had entered the ramparts quaintly bethinking himself unobserved, and was tenanting a room immediately above the suspected philanderer. This snooper was resourceful. He contrived to make it known that he had bribed the colored waiter to give him a duplicate key of the pseudo-lover's apartment. At his leisure and his ease he could penetrate this mysterious domain and appropriate any articles or documents that he imagined to be of any importance, however remote.

For several months he was a high-class guest, paying presumably high-class prices, which were defrayed by the equally high-class Mr. "X." Remember the Platonic dictum: "Suckers sustain snoopers" as well as the Aristotelian apothegm: "Beat a bum to the bank." Thus our detective friend was at all times familiar with the idioms, albeit with none of the ideologies of the ancient Greek Philosophers. . . .

The delicate icing on the birthday cake was the lady in the case, sleutheress, siren histrion. Proceeding upon the long since discarded theory that "men prefer blondes" she was super-peroxided, tall, opulent, and might have been alluring were she not so intimately reminiscent of the Scandanavian Peninsula.

But she was fertile, albeit futile inasmuch as one evening, simulating with Aristopha[n]ic fidelity a blousey bloater, she affected to be drunk, fell against Galatea's door, told Galatea how beautiful she was, admitted a wee drop too much, thought to hear a baby's voice within, expressed a maudlin sentimentality for infants, wished she had one herself or at least bravely hoped to and pleaded for a peek at the little innocent; all for the quite obvious purpose of inspecting the suspected apartment, and observing the lay of the land. But Galatea, fancying the lady's taste might be warped by whiskey and not caring overmuch for apparently bibulous intruders, finally closed the door and left Scandanavia to her further devices.

But protean was our snooperette. Two evenings later she was parading the Avenue, spotted the suspected philanderer, winked convulsively, sighed heavily, and then rushed suddenly into a book-shop, ostensibly to purchase a newspaper which she forgot, however, to take from the counter, but rather rushed incontinentally to the public phone-booth obviously to report the dramatic rencontre; all whereof was quickly and unobtrusively observed by the ingenuous victim, who walked leisurely away, but not I fear, impressed by woman's wiles, guiles, or other sinister forces.

Well, this concludes the first act. Methinks the drama attempted to be staged by Mr. "X" requires a new plot, a new script, a new caste [sic], and certainly a new author.

In January 1940, based on the slender evidence gathered by the "Scandanavian snooperette," Janet sued Jack Bouvier for divorce on the grounds of adultery, informing the press of her charges. Subsequently, on a Friday in early January, photographs of Janet, Jacqueline, and Lee appeared in four New York papers in connection with the suit. Thanks to syndication, the picture and the notice of the divorce suit were soon in almost every city in the country. Here is the text in the January 26, 1940, issue of the *New York Daily Mirror:*

SOCIETY BROKER SUED FOR DIVORCE

A line in the Social Register will be cracked right in two if Mrs. Janet Lee Bouvier of 1 Gracie Square has her way. Mrs. Bouvier asks alimony and custody of two children, Jacqueline and Caroline. Mrs. Bouvier claims the society broker who lives at 765 Park [Jack was then temporarily living with his father] was overfriendly with another socialite,

Marjorie Berrien, as well as with unnamed women in his summer home in East Hampton.

Janet's reckless publishing of these particular unfounded charges of adultery against her husband caused serious damage to Jack Bouvier's reputation in New York, resulting in far fewer invitations to parties and balls. It had a devastating effect on their two daughters as well. At Miss Chapin's School, Jacqueline had to put up with the snickers of her schoolmates. And at Sunday and holiday luncheons at Grandfather Bouvier's, she had to contend with a few snide remarks from the cousins, although Jack himself soon put an end to them.

Still, it was difficult for the ten-year-old girl to bear. She suddenly was the daughter of a black sheep, a man in disrepute, an adulterer. It was all over the papers, all over the country. Jacqueline felt terribly ashamed. From now on, she craved one thing: respectability, the rehabilitation of her family's image. She had to find a way to remedy the embarrassment of her parents' divorce.

Later, Janet, her father, and their lawyers were unable to make their sensational charges stick, and the suit for divorce on the grounds of adultery was eventually dropped. Although the charges had been published nationwide, their dismissal had not. Jack was so humiliated and outraged he agreed to a quickie Nevada divorce. As soon as she could, Janet flew off to Reno with the children.

Chapter Three

The Divorce

It was in early June 1940 that Janet, Jacqueline, and Lee took up temporary residence at the Lazy "A" Bar Ranch on the outskirts of Reno. Jacqueline was in her element at the ranch. The ten-year-old tomboy rode a horse named Jim her first day, but soon gave him up for a wilder mount, a mustang pony named Banjo, and then an even peppier horse called Wagstaff. While Janet was in town meeting with her lawyer and making appearances in divorce court, Jacqueline was thundering over the Nevada desert on western-style saddles with pommels atop a kind of mount she had never ridden before.

When she wasn't riding, Jacqueline was splashing around in the hot-spring pool or reveling in the state's lack of a speed limit as she tore down the Nevada highways at ninety miles per hour with an occasional guest at the ranch who was only too happy to offer the lovely young girl a joy ride. Her father had given her a love of the excitement of fast cars; he liked to drive his girls at top speed in his Mercury convertible down the highway from East Hampton to Montauk. Peppy horses and fast cars were the great youthful passions of the woman who one day would project an image of femininity, grace, and refinement to the world.

Meanwhile, Jack Bouvier was pining for his beloved daughters, especially Jacqueline, as he shuttled back and forth between New York and East Hampton making arrangements for their return from Nevada in August. He was pleased to inform Jacqueline that Danseuse was still in excellent shape and that he was entering Jackie in the East Hampton Horse Show for Juniors with equitation, jumping, and family classes.

I recall my father telling me that Uncle Jack had confided that East Hampton held little attraction without Jackie and Lee there. By the summer of 1940, Jack's love for his daughter Jacqueline had become an obsessive passion. It was a special love of a father for his daughter, the likes of which I have never witnessed in America before or since. At Bouvier family gatherings, it was almost embarrassing to hear Jack extol Jacqueline's qualities before everyone. To see Jack and Jacqueline strolling along Park Avenue arm in arm was to behold two lovers who delighted in each other's company. Only in southern France and Italy have I observed such closeness between father and daughter. As Jack wrote to Jacqueline at the Lazy "A" Bar Ranch, only she gave him the feeling his life was "worthwhile living." Jacqueline reciprocated this closeness without reserve or embarrassment. I never saw her try to conceal the deep love she had for her father.

I now believe that Jack Bouvier could emotionally afford to live the life he led after his divorce—unmarried, but with a harem of young girls at his beck and call—because he didn't *need* one steady love in his life. He already had one—Jacqueline.

The intense love between father and daughter would continue to fuel the rivalry with Janet for Jacqueline's time and affections to the point where it would become agonizing for all concerned.

In mid-July 1940, when Janet was on the verge of pocketing her longed-for divorce decree and Jacqueline was about to turn eleven, Jack triumphantly wrote Jacqueline that he had rented a house for the month of August very near the East Hampton Riding Club. Her favorite dog, Caprice, and favorite horse, Danseuse, would be waiting.

This was enough to persuade Jacqueline and Lee to make sure they would appear in East Hampton promptly on August 1, which they did, leaving their mother behind with her divorce decree at her Gracie Square apartment. Janet would spend the rest of the summer alone in New York, occasionally weekending in East Hampton with her parents, who were delighted with the way things had turned out. Finally, that irresponsible rascal, Jack Bouvier, was out of their daughter's life.

Jack's reunion with his girls was all that he hoped. Jacqueline loved the house he had rented next to the Riding Club, and as soon as she had unpacked her bags, she tore over to the club's stables to be with Danseuse.

Three days later, Jack brought his daughters to Lasata for his twin sisters' birthday on August 4. It was as if nothing had ever happened. The entire Bouvier family was once again happily reunited. Of course, everyone missed Grandmother Bouvier, who had died in April, causing Grampy Jack and his son to wear black armbands on their jacket sleeves. The birthday turned out to be a joyous occasion, with the reading of many poems and speeches and, as usual, Big Edie leading the birthday song with her customary gusto.

Soon Jacqueline was back in competition at the East End horse shows and Jack was able to boast to everyone that Jackie had "cleaned up" at the East Hampton Horse Show, winning every event she entered, including equitation and jumping for girls and boys under twenty. The *East Hampton Star,* the *Southampton Press,* and the *Social Spectator* trumpeted her victories. Jacqueline Bouvier had, at the tender age of eleven, begun to achieve a measure of fame on eastern Long Island.

To add to Jacqueline's enjoyment that summer, Jack invited George de Mohrenschildt for a couple of weekends. I remember how much Jacqueline enjoyed his company and how I used to watch them ride in the fence-enclosed ring in back of Lasata, from which Janet was now excluded. Jacqueline and the Baron, as we called him, took the fences with gusto, laughing and shouting at each other in front of an audience of all the other grandchildren.

By this time, Jacqueline had developed a preference for the company of adults over that of her peers, among the Bouvier grandchildren she was in a category by herself. She was a champion equestrienne, the apple of her father's and grandfather's eyes, and she hung out with grown-up men like de Mohrenschildt.

Now that Jack was divorced, he was free to again take up his libertine ways and his interrupted career as a Don Juan extraordinaire. Jack's conquests would occasionally appear at the Bouvier cabana at the Maidstone Beach Club to change for a swim. One I vividly remember was Mrs. Anne Plugge, the wife of a British Army Officer temporarily attached to the Pentagon. Their romance would last until the end of the war in 1945 and eventually threaten to be a major embarrassment for Jacqueline when she became First Lady.

Before long, summer was over and Jacqueline and Lee returned to their mother's New York apartment while Jack went back to his room in the Westbury Hotel. Now Jack could enjoy the company of his daughters only on Saturday afternoons and Sundays until 6 P.M.

In early October, Jacqueline resumed her studies at Miss Chapin's School and, having overcome her rambunctious period, did so well that Headmistress Stringfellow told Janet Bouvier: "I mightn't have kept Jacqueline—except that she has the most inquiring mind we've had in this school in thirty-five years."

Despite her success at school, Jacqueline began neglecting her father by not phoning him regularly. This tendency, which was only adolescent carelessness, drew a sharp rebuke from Jack Bouvier on November 1 when he wrote her a stern letter reminding her of her responsibility and asking her to phone him if he hadn't called her by 7:30 P.M. He further reminded her that he had not fought her mother and grandmother Lee for fair custody of her and her sister only to have his daughters not care enough to phone him. And he lamented what he saw as her and her sister's lack of attention and confessed that he felt "a bit neglected by my two dear ones." His complaint would be repeated frequently during the

Jack Bouvier with his daughters Jacqueline and Lee in Central Park in the winter of 1941. Every weekend Jack would take his daughters out for a romp in the park.

next twelve years as he felt his hold on his beloved daughters gradually slipping away.

It took a major victory of Jacqueline's in an important horse show for Jack to snap out of the funk he had fallen into because of his daughters' alleged neglect. During the summer, Jacqueline had won two top prizes at East End horse shows: the A.S.P.C.A. Alfred Maclay Trophy for Horsemanship and the A.S.P.C.A. Good Hands event. These victories made her eligible to enter the final runoff at the Madison Square Garden Horse Show.

Jacqueline scored a complete triumph in the Madison Square Garden finals by beating a field of twenty young riders, both boys and girls. The *New York Times* reported on the event:

Jacqueline Bouvier, an eleven year old equestrienne from East Hampton, Long Island, scored a double victory in the horsemanship competition. Miss Bouvier achieved a rare distinction. The occasions are few when a young rider wins both contests in the same show.

At the age of eleven, Jacqueline had overcome the endless wrangling between her mother and father over the past five years, the disruptions of her life imposed by the separation agreement and the divorce decree, to become a hardworking, straight-A student and a fearless leader in her favorite sport. Adversity had given her a toughness of character that would serve her well in the years to come.

At Grandfather Bouvier's sumptuous Thanksgiving and Christmas feasts, I can recall how Jacqueline was now treated as someone special. She held a position in the family apart from her other little cousins. Of course, she was still friendly with us all. But her much-publicized victories at national championships, combined with feelings of shame over her parents' divorce, had made her somewhat remote and secretive. These traits became more and more pronounced as she grew older, until her fame transformed her into something of a national enigma—a much admired woman, a real-life tragic heroine, whose personality was nevertheless unfathomable.

Chapter Four

The Remarriage

*A*lthough Janet Bouvier took great pride in Jacqueline's equestrian achievements, which were in large part due to her training and example, she was uncomfortable and at loose ends during the winter of 1940–1941. Here she was, a thirty-four-year-old divorcée, living and raising two young children on an alimony of $1,050 a month—not much for the social position she had to maintain—with no skills or assets other than her own ability as a champion equestrienne and her still-intact attractiveness as a female. She knew she had to find a new husband, a special one, one who would be very rich and rode horses. But where to find him?

It became an all-consuming search. Janet's life evolved into a seemingly endless succession of luncheons, teas, cocktail parties, dinner parties, dances, nightclub soirees, and weekend house parties in search of Mr. Right.

My mother and my Aunt Michelle used to joke incessantly about what they called The Great Manhunt, reporting their findings about Janet's new beaus back to their brother. When they learned that Janet was frequently seen in the company of a wealthy financier named Zinsser, they used to giggle about Janet going from A to Z in her search. When, for some unknown reason, Janet and Zinsser broke up and Janet was compelled to resume hunting,

The Champion. Jacqueline Bouvier shows exceptional determination and form as she and her favorite horse, Danseuse, clear a fence at an East Hampton horse show on August 30, 1941.

she eventually, after a protracted chase, landed in the arms of the twice-divorced Hugh D. Auchincloss Jr., and the twins chortled that, after going from A to Z, she went back from Z to A.

Two years after her Reno divorce, Janet finally ensnared a new mate—and what a catch he was. Hughdie, as he was called, was a multimillionaire investment banker who had inherited an enormous fortune from his mother. He owned two vast country properties, a seventy-five-acre estate in Newport, Hammersmith Farm, overlooking Narragansett Bay, in which he spent his summers, and Merrywood, a forty-six-acre estate, in McLean, Virginia, with a view of the Potomac, where he wintered. And he actually owned horses and rode them.

Janet Bouvier with her daughter Jacqueline, twelve, and Lee, ten, going to an East Hampton wedding in 1941.

The Auchinclosses were a large and distinguished clan of Scottish origin (the first Auchincloss came over from Paisley in 1803). None had ever made a fortune of his own, but they all had a knack for marrying into some of America's wealthiest families. Various Auchincloss males had allied themselves to the Saltonstalls, the Van Rensselaers, the du Ponts, the Tiffanys, the Vanderbilts, the Jenningses, and the Rockefellers.

Hughdie's mother, the former Emma Brewster Jennings, was the daughter of Oliver B. Jennings, one of the original founding partners, along with John D. Rockefeller Sr., of Standard Oil. Before she died, she gave to her son $1 million, which he used to purchase what came to be known as the investment banking firm of Auchincloss, Redpath, and Parker, based in Washington. She left him still more millions in her will.

After a brief honeymoon, Janet became the third mistress of Hammersmith Farm and Merrywood. The first one had been Maya Charapovitsky, daughter of a Russian czarist naval officer, with whom Hughdie had a son, Hugh D. Auchincloss III, known as Yusha. After divorcing Maya in 1935, Hughdie had married Nina Gore Vidal, daughter of T.B. Gore, the noted blind senator from Oklahoma, and mother, by her first marriage, of the eminent author, Gore Vidal, then known as Eugene Vidal Jr. Hughdie then fathered two more children, a daughter, Nina, known as Nini, and another son, Thomas, known as Tommy.

In his sardonic memoir of his last days in the Auchincloss family, *Reflections on Glory Reflected,* Gore Vidal wrote that after his mother left Merrywood "for Love," Hughdie "was promptly married for his money by one of her ladies-in-waiting, who brought him two very poor but very adorable frizzy-haired step-daughters to take my place in his ample heart." In other words, when Gore Vidal and his mother moved out, Janet, Jacqueline, and Lee moved in. Jacqueline occupied Gore Vidal's bedroom at Merrywood. Soon Janet would solidify her place in the Auchincloss household by producing two more children, Janet Jr., born in 1945, when Hughdie was 57 and Janet 39, and James, born two years later.

Jacqueline (top left) with her new family, the Auchinclosses, in a 1945 Christmas photo. Janet Lee Bouvier had married Hugh D. Auchincloss Jr. of Newport and Washington in 1942. Sitting next to Jacqueline is her new stepbrother, Hugh D. "Yusha" Auchincloss III. In the middle row from left to right are Nina and Thomas Auchincloss and Lee Bouvier. Janet is seated in front with her new baby, Janet Jennings Auchincloss, Jacqueline's new half-sister.

By 1947, Jacqueline found herself part of a family consisting of a sister, two stepbrothers, one stepsister, one half-sister, and a half-brother—seven siblings in all.

Gore Vidal did not have much use for his stepfather; he called Hughdie "a bulky man who stammered," was "slothful," and *"was unable to do work of any kind"* [emphasis Vidal's]. Others found Auchincloss staid, unimaginative, boring, and frequently absent-minded. I thought him stuffy and uncommunicative; he often mumbled in conversation. Although he was humorless man, he did have a number of quirky aspects to his personality. He was an avid collector of pornography, and, even though he was immensely rich, he hated to spend money on such trifles as electricity; he was forever scolding his family and servants for not turning off the lights.

Jackie and Lee did not feel an instant rapport toward him, and they were resented by Nina Gore Vidal Auchincloss as unwanted intruders, but gradually they began to tolerate his stodginess—at least he wasn't mean-spirited—and eventually came to appreciate the life he and his money provided.

Janet found him stable, reliable, and calm, attributes somewhat lacking in her first husband. She was willing to put up with his inherent dullness for the peace of mind and purse he gave her.

Years later, Jacqueline wrote an appreciative note to her mother and stepfather on their tenth wedding anniversary. She noted how they could all have been "separate units" but instead were united as a family by what they had shared and been given.

As for Jack Bouvier, his assessment of Hughdie Auchincloss was more in line with Gore Vidal's. Not long after Janet's remarriage, he began circulating an admonition on the floor of the New York Stock Exchange that he vainly hoped would put a dent in Hughdie's business: "Take a loss with Auchincloss." And he took prompt measures to re-cement his beloved daughters to his own family. No sooner were Jacqueline and Lee installed at Hammersmith Farm in late June 1942 than he summoned them to East Hampton, telling them their horses were being well taken care of

at the stables of the East Hampton Riding Club and under no circumstances would he allow them to be shipped to Newport.

Jacqueline and Lee were happy to return to their old summer
haunts. Their father had rented a house on the dunes so they could
take an early morning swim before giving the horses their daily
workout. For Jack, the situation was ideal. He finally had his darling girls all to himself, with no interference from Janet. He also
had his British love, Anne Plugge, up for the month of August;
she joined the merry household, while her army officer husband
toiled endless hours in the wartime Pentagon.

To Jack's delight, his daughters took a shine to Anne Plugge
and before long they were doing everything together: swimming,
riding, going to parties, and even joining all of us at Lasata. There
Grandfather, aunts, and cousins welcomed Jack's British lady friend
as practically one of the family. Never once did I sense that Jackie
or Lee disapproved of their father's relationship with Mrs. Plugge
or were embarrassed by its evident passion.

As a boy of only thirteen I recall what a torrid affair they
enjoyed. I used to watch them excitedly as they necked on the
beach just beyond the Maidstone Club's precincts; one day I stumbled across them in a wild embrace on the slatted floor of the
men's shower room in the Bouvier cabana.

Needless to say, Jack Bouvier enjoyed a glorious summer in
1942. Both his girls and his lover were with him, and *Janet was
nowhere in sight.*

Inevitably, fall arrived, and this time Jacqueline and Lee were
compelled to join their mother and the Auchincloss family at
Merrywood outside Washington, far from Jack's reach. Jacqueline
withdrew from Miss Chapin's School and entered a Washington day
school, Holton-Arms, for the fall and winter terms. For Jack, that
meant no more weekend romps with his girls and their dogs and
horses in Central Park, no more chocolate sundaes with them at
Schrafft's, and no more shared Sunday luncheons at Grampy Jack's.

Above all, it meant that Jack would not have his girls for
Thanksgiving. He complained to them in a November letter that it

Jacqueline, now a physically strong young teenager, leading Danseuse from the stables at Lasata. For a change she is wearing a dress, not her riding habit, which reveals the muscularity of her legs.

would be their first separation on that day since they were born, and told them the entire Bouvier family was going to have Thanksgiving dinner at Gramps's. They would miss many poems, including seven that Gramps had written for the occasion.

Jack would also be lacking the company of Mrs. Plugge. Her husband, who had been at Sea Island Beach for three weeks, was due back in New York on Thanksgiving. But he wasn't completely disheartened. Since the Colonel would not be returning to England until spring, Mrs. Plugge would still be around for a while.

Nevertheless, Jack made a pathetic plea telling his daughters that he missed them very much and that his only satisfaction is when he talks with them by phone or receives letters from them. He reminded Jacqueline that, since she was the eldest, it was up to her to write him and have Lee do the same—"that is if you care enough about your father to do so—sometimes I wonder."

Unfortunately for Jack, Jacqueline took an instant liking to her new winter home. Merrywood, with its great Georgian-style, ivy-clad brick mansion, was spacious enough to allow her privacy, and its position high on a bluff overlooking the Potomac from the Virginia side gave her a feeling of calm and security. The estate, with its bright green meadows, stables, riding paths, clumps of forest, and magnificent views of the Potomac, was a far cry from 1 Gracie Square and Jack's room in the Westbury. Gore Vidal, who spent six years at Merrywood, described life there as "peaceful . . . a bit Henry Jamesian, a world of deliberate quietude removed from the twentieth-century tension. It was a life that gave total security, but not much preparation for the real world."

Jack Bouvier was made aware of the serene beauty of Merrywood by Jacqueline, a bit tactlessly, who proclaimed the estate's charms to her father in letters and over the phone, and it depressed him that he had so much less to offer his girls, at least during the fall–winter season. According to my father, Jack often became despondent during the winter of 1942–1943 over the apparent loss of his daughters to the Auchinclosses, and took to drinking excessively. But he never gave up. He was fully aware that he now had a powerful and dangerous rival in Hugh D. Auchincloss

Jacqueline, in full riding habit, standing between her father, Jack Bouvier (left), and a very proud grandfather, Major Bouvier, in a paddock near the riding ring and stables at Lasata, East Hampton, 1943. Jacqueline is now fourteen years old.

for the time and affections of his daughters and was prepared to go to almost any length to do battle with him.

By the time Jacqueline reached her fourteenth birthday in the summer of 1943, she had begun to exploit this rivalry to her advantage. To goad Daddy into acceding to her wishes, she would tell him something positive about Mummy and Uncle Hughdie. To get a favor out of Mummy, all she had to do was mention something nice about Daddy. The consequences of this divided and highly contentious family life made Jacqueline much smarter and shrewder than she would have been had her parents not divorced and her mother not remarried.

Jacqueline had already proved herself a leader in horse show contests and in the classroom with her consistent straight-A averages. Now she began to add another dimension to her accomplishments. She became a master of personal relations, possessing a mysterious authority that would compel people to do her bidding. I have a very distinct memory of this ability, dating from our mid-teens. If, when we were at the Bouvier cabana at the Maidstone, another cousin asked me to go to the cafeteria and bring back a hamburger and a soft drink, I would tell the cousin "Go get it yourself." If Jacqueline asked, I would rush down the boardwalk to get her what she wanted without hesitation, as if my mother or sister had asked me. I felt that close to her.

We all were aware of Aunt Janet's remarriage to Hugh D. Auchincloss and Jacqueline's and Lee's new lives. Uncle Jack used to tell us what a stuffed shirt Mr. Auchincloss was and comment on what "a rotten time" Jacqueline and Lee were having at Hammersmith Farm and Merrywood. He would even ridicule Jacqueline's new stepbrother, Yusha, calling him Yusha Poosha. We took all of this with a grain of salt. But if we raised the issue of her new family with Jacqueline, we would be met with a chilling silence. As before, and more so now, she was close-mouthed about that part of her life—you could never get anything personal out of her. She kept all her feelings bottled up, a tendency we continued to see for the rest of her existence.

Chapter Five

A Divided Life

After a winter of sulking over his daughters' living with the stuffy Auchinclosses in faraway Merrywood, Jack Bouvier bounced back in the summer of 1944 when his girls rejoined him in East Hampton. Jacqueline had just turned fifteen and Lee was eleven. Jack was delighted when a diplomatic Jacqueline told him Uncle Hughdie wasn't as much fun to be with as Daddy and that she and Lee had trouble "fitting in" with the Auchincloss children.

And so the pattern of Jacqueline's family life was set. For ten years, from 1943 to 1953, the year she married John F. Kennedy, she would lead a divided life, the object of a tug-of-war between the Auchinclosses of Washington and Newport and the Bouviers of Manhattan and East Hampton. That decade was punctuated by a trip to Europe in the summer of 1947, a school year at the Sorbonne in 1949–1950 and another summer trip to Europe with her sister Lee in 1951.

When Jacqueline arrived in East Hampton that summer, we all noticed the changes that had taken place in her body and personality since the previous summer. I remember when she first came to the Bouvier cabana. She was now a tall young teenager, with breasts, hips, and a touch of lipstick. Boys suddenly started admiring her and took to hanging around the cabana, waiting for her to come out.

"Is Jackie in there?" one of them would call, and Jackie would whisper loudly to me from the ladies' dressing compartment: "Jack, tell them to *go away,* that I'm not here."

Jacqueline would have nothing to do with boys her own age, or even with young men ten years older. She preferred the company of much older men. Her favorite at the time was another White Russian émigré, Prince Serge Obolensky, who was about the same age as her father and worked as a public relations man in New York for the city's most luxurious hotels. Not that she was sexually attracted to such men as Prince Serge—I believe Jacqueline did not become sexually active until she was in her early twenties—she just enjoyed their company more. She learned more from older men, certainly a lot more than what the young spoiled brats who spent their summers lounging around on the sands of Maidstone Beach could tell her. And so she would inform us proudly that she went for a drive with Serge to Montauk Point and he told her what it was like in Old Russia before the Bolsheviks and that one of his uncles had served at the court of Czar Nicholas II!

Jacqueline never lost the interest in Russia that Baron George de Mohrenshildt and Prince Serge Obolensky instilled in her as a young teenager. One of the first books she edited at Viking Press after the death of her second husband Aristotle Onassis was *In the Russian Style,* a lavishly illustrated coffee-table book on the artistic splendors of Imperial Russia.

Once again, life at Lasata in 1944 unfolded as before. Jacqueline and Lee spent their afternoons tearing around the riding ring with their adoring grandfather and father looking on. Jacqueline had become the undisputed champion equestrienne of her age group in Long Island's East End, having won all the shows in Southampton, East Hampton, Bridgehampton, and Smithtown. Lasata's sunken hedge-enclosed Italian flower garden was, thanks to Paul

Yuska, the Polish gardener, as radiant as ever. The mossy old fountain at the far end still sprayed its incandescent mist into the summer air. The baroque French shepherdesses still guarded the brick pathways to the tennis court and the other gardens, orchards, and cornfields. But now three Bouviers were missing from the long oak dining-room table watched over by the ancestral portraits.

The war in Europe and the Pacific was hurtling toward its final outcome—the Allies had landed on the beaches of Normandy on June 6 and soon American troops would be arriving in the Philippines' Leyte Gulf—and three Bouviers were in uniform. Michel Bouvier was an army officer waiting for his orders to be sent overseas; Phelan Beale was an army officer seeing combat in the Pacific; and Bouvier Beale was a radio technician in the thick of the fighting in Burma.

Nevertheless, Grandfather Bouvier, who even in the inferno of the August heat still wore his high, starched collars, was in good spirits as he surveyed his diminished brood devouring the luscious fruits of his gardens. He launched into a speech extolling the military valor of his family from the Revolutionary War, through the Civil War, World War I, and now the final showdown with Hitler and Hirohito. I recall that Grampy Jack was, to the end of his days, always very much the CEO of the Bouvier family. Always in full command, he laid down the law for the household and no one would dare cross him.

Sometimes, after these Sunday luncheons, Jacqueline did not immediately make a beeline to the stables, but would stroll through the gardens of Lasata with me and perhaps another cousin. She and I were aware of, and very sensitive to, its overwhelming beauty in mid-summer. We had imbibed that beauty for fifteen years, and it had formed our visual taste for the rest of our lives. It certainly contributed not a little to Jacqueline's celebrated sense of style. The Bouvier family ethos was so unlike the Kennedy world Jacqueline would one day marry into. Ours was primarily concerned with beauty, style, individualism, and enjoyment instead of the fierce, and ultimately disastrous, will to power that fueled the Kennedy family ethos.

John H. Davis, fourteen, enjoying the glories of Lasata in August 1943. Jacqueline and I were particularly sensitive to the overwhelming beauty of the estate, which, more than any other influence, formed our taste and sense of style for the rest of our lives.

Another change in Jacqueline's personality that we began to observe when she entered her mid-teens was the emergence of her droll sense of humor. It found permanent expression in the book she and Lee wrote and illustrated about their trip to Europe in the summer of 1951, *One Special Summer*. It was also at this time that Jacqueline began to develop that unique breathless, whispery manner of speech that fooled so many people into thinking she was either stupid or playing innocent.

During the summer of 1944, Jack Bouvier enjoyed a wonderful August with his girls and, as before, loved showing them off at the Maidstone Club and sharing their riding triumphs. With Janet up at Newport becoming the chatelaine of Hammersmith Farm, he felt much more free to be himself. However, there were those inevitable moments at the Maidstone when he accidentally ran into Janet's father, Old Man Lee, and would have to endure his withering scowl.

It was also in that summer that Jack heard from his British wartime love, Anne Plugge, that she had given birth to twins, a boy and a girl, who could not possibly have been Colonel Plugge's. What transpired between them after Jack learned this news is not known. We do know that five years later, when Jacqueline was attending the Sorbonne, she finally met the Plugge twins on a brief trip to England and realized they were her half-brother and half-sister. But that is another story and we will come to it later.

That fall, after a brief stay with her mother and the Auchinclosses at Hammersmith Farm, Jacqueline entered Miss Porter's boarding school in Farmington, Connecticut, and began her three-year preparation for college. Attending Miss Porter's had become a Bouvier tradition. Jacqueline's twin aunts, Maude and Michelle, had gone there, as had her older cousin Little Edie Beale. She was accompanied to

Farmington by her cousin, Shella Scott, Aunt Michelle's daughter, who was the same age.

After she pleaded with Grampy Jack to let Danseuse board in Farmington's stables for the winter, he agreed to pay the cost: $50 a month. During her first year, Jacqueline roomed with Sue Norton, a tall blonde from a distinguished New England family. In her second and third years, she roomed with Nancy Tuckerman, known as Tucky, a stocky brunette from a Long Island family that had known the Bouviers for years, who had been a classmate at Miss Chapin's. Nancy Tuckerman became Jacqueline's closest friend, helpmate, and confidante, the faithful keeper of all, or almost all, her secrets. She would one day work for her in the White House, follow her to Doubleday, and even play a role after her death in settling her estate.

According to her cousin Shella, Jacqueline thrived at Farmington, although she never became one of the girls. She sacrificed participating in school athletics to working out with Danseuse and teaching the horse how to pull a sleigh in the snow. She studied hard, earning an A− average, and especially enjoyed her courses in art history and English literature, which fueled her lifelong interest in painting, sculpture, architecture, and Shakespeare. She also worked on the school newspaper, *The Salamagundy,* contributing stories, poems, and delightful cartoons, the precursors of those she would one day publish in *One Special Summer.* And she put her Bouvier histrionic ability to good use by performing in school plays.

One of the high points in her life at Farmington was the arrival of her father for a weekend visit. Jacqueline loved to show off her handsome, dashing Daddy, with his perennial deep tan and beautifully custom-tailored double-breasted suits. And Black Jack Bouvier always made a big hit. He would revel in the adulation of his daughter's friends, who treated him like a movie-star and remarked how much he resembled Clark Gable, and he would reciprocate by taking a half dozen of them with Jacqueline to the Elm Tree Inn for expensive luncheons of steak and ice cream.

Jack Bouvier was delighted to have Jacqueline at Miss Porter's, even though her tuition was, in his words, "pretty steep," because it effectively kept her out of the Auchincloss orbit during the school year. By her second year, Jack had given up his hotel room and settled in a comfortable two-bedroom apartment at 125 East 74th Street. The second bedroom was reserved for Jacqueline when she came down to New York on weekends—which, as it turned out, was not often, since the school discouraged students from leaving on weekends. At least it was better than having her stay at Merrywood seven days a week.

└> There were, however, events taking place in the Auchincloss family that demanded Jacqueline's time and attention. In the winter of 1945, Janet Auchincloss gave birth to a daughter, Janet Jennings Auchincloss. Jacqueline attended Janet Jr.'s christening in Washington and wrote a poem commemorating the event in which she expressed her delight in having a new baby girl in the Auchincloss fold.

The acquisition of a new baby sister brought out Jacqueline's maternal instincts, perhaps for the first time. She mothered the little girl as if she were her own child and grew very fond of her. The relationship between the two was, in a sense, a rehearsal for Jacqueline's role as a mother. With Janet Jr. Jacqueline discovered a powerful side of her personality she never knew she had up to that time, for Jacqueline the glamor girl was to become a very maternal woman who passionately loved children.

Jacqueline grew closer to Janet Jr., a charming, delightful girl, than she did to any of the other Auchincloss children. In 1966 she made a special trip from Hawaii, where she had been vacationing, to Hammersmith Farm to attend Janet Jr.'s wedding to Lewis Rutherford.

Not long after her marriage, Janet Rutherford developed cancer. She died of the disease at age thirty-nine. At her funeral service, Jacqueline offered this eulogy:

Knowing Janet was like having a cardinal in your garden.
She was bright and lovely and incredibly alive.

Several momentous world events occurred that spring. On April 12 President Roosevelt died of a cerebral hemorrhage, and on May 7 Germany surrendered to the Allies and Hitler killed himself. The death of FDR did not disturb the staunchly Republican Bouvier family very much. Grandfather Bouvier often complained that FDR was taxing the family out of existence, and Jack Bouvier had loathed the man, claiming that FDR's Securities and Exchange Commission made it impossible for him to make a decent living. Of course, everyone in the family rejoiced over Germany's surrender. It meant that Lt. Michel Bouvier, the family heir and Jacqueline's godfather, would not have to go to war in Europe. Instead, he married and produced two sons, Michel Bouvier IV and John Vernou Bouvier IV, who would carry on the Bouvier name.

In August, the Bouviers held their summer reunion at Lasata once again, with Jacqueline and Lee arriving a bit late from Hammersmith Farm. I remember that summer vividly because of one event: the dropping of the atomic bomb on Hiroshima on August 6, two days after the birthday of my mother and her twin sister. I was very interested in science and had been studying scientists' efforts to smash the atom at school during the previous winter. One of my jobs at Lasata was to bike into town in the early morning and bring back the *New York Times* to Grampy Jack. I was both astonished and keenly interested in the atomic explosion that had apparently leveled Hiroshima and found that the only person in the Bouvier family who took a similar interest was Grandfather, who, among his many essays, had written of Mach, J. J. Thompson, Rutherford, and Einstein. No one else in the family seemed at all captivated by this event. I recall that what the family was most interested in was the softball game to be held that afternoon between Jack Bouvier's Black Ducks and Kip Farrington's Mugwumps.

The summer of 1945 did not prove a satisfying one for Jack insofar as his relations with his daughters were concerned. After Danseuse triumphed at the East Hampton horse show, the horse suffered a serious fall and injured one of her hind legs. Jacqueline wanted her father to ship her to Newport, but he refused. Jack feared that losing control of Jacqueline's beloved mare would mean losing

Newport, 1945. A sixteen-year-old Jacqueline Bouvier vamps for the camera at the Newport Tennis Club.

control of his daughter. Annoyed at her father's intransigence, a head-strong Jacqueline cut short her stay in East Hampton and returned early to Hammersmith Farm. Jack sensed that she was becoming more adjusted to living with the Auchinclosses and it distressed him. Although he refused to send Danseuse to Newport, he agreed to transport her to Farmington and pay for her upkeep as well.

Where to keep Danseuse continued to be a contentious issue between father and daughter well into 1946. In May, Jacqueline asked Jack to ship the horse to Newport, where she would be well cared for by two Portuguese grooms and a coachman.

Jack put his foot down and wrote Jacqueline to "give the horse a chance," adding that, since they both loved her, he was willing to spend $500 on Danseuse for the summer because the mare deserved closely supervised dry and wet rubdowns, long walks, regularly scheduled exercising, grassing, and hot mashes. Only he and her grooms in East Hampton could guarantee this.

He further told her she would not find the time to do all that was necessary for the ailing horse in Newport, and urged her to devote her summer to the recreations she loved most—swimming, tennis, golf, and automobiles—and not wear herself out feeding, conditioning, and exercising Danseuse.

Then, with a certain sarcasm, Jack continued his letter: "Next summer you can take her to Newport for keeps and make her a household pet if you want." But, for the current summer, he demanded that the mare stay at East Hampton, so she would be in good condition for Jacqueline's last year at Farmington. He further admonished her to be more considerate of the horse responsible for making her one of the best riders of her age group on Long Island.

There wasn't much Jacqueline could do to counter that argument, so Danseuse remained in East Hampton during the summer of 1946 and was shipped to Farmington in the fall. Jack had scored a minor victory over the Auchinclosses.

Jacqueline graduated from Miss Porter's School in June 1947. In the class yearbook, she was characterized as being most known for

A formal portrait of Jacqueline Bouvier upon her graduation from Miss Porter's School in Farmington, Connecticut, in 1947.

her "Wit," most usually found "Laughing with Tucky," and having the ambition "Not to be a Housewife."

There followed two coming-out parties in Newport for Jacqueline to which Jack Bouvier was, of course, not invited. In that old-fashioned milieu, more evocative of the nineteenth century than the twentieth, young women from wealthy families were supposed to be formally introduced to Society—to "come out"— at the age of eighteen. The first party, in June, was a tea to celebrate not only Jacqueline's debut in Newport Society but also the christening of her new five-month-old half-brother, James Lee Auchincloss, known as Jamie. The tea, an afternoon reception with dancing, was attended by three hundred guests, most of whom Jacqueline already knew. It was held at Hammersmith Farm.

The second was a more traditional debutante party, a formal dinner dance at Newport's old Clambake Club that took place in mid-July about two weeks before Jacqueline was due to turn eighteen and visit her father in East Hampton. Jacqueline made her formal debut along with a family friend her same age, Rose Grosvenor, daughter of the Theodore Grosvenors, who were distant Auchincloss relatives. To my knowledge, no members of the Bouvier family, other than Jacqueline's sister Lee, were invited. Jacqueline now inhabited two totally separate and distinct family milieus: the Auchinclosses, to whom she was now related by blood, with an Auchincloss half-sister and half-brother, and the Bouviers, whom she was destined to see less and less, to the acute distress of her father and, I might add, many of her cousins, including myself. *began her divided life... life in spotlight/ private*

Jacqueline did come to East Hampton in August 1947 to be with her father and nurse the now ailing Danseuse. She also turned up at Lasata for one of our ritual August feasts. By this time Grandfather Bouvier was seriously ill with prostate cancer and was unable to celebrate the twins' birthday on August 4. However, he felt well enough to preside over his own birthday on August 14. It was his eighty-second, and he noted in his diary that he addressed a few remarks to his grandchildren. I dimly recall that birthday party because it was the last one held at Lasata. Grampy Jack died five

Jacqueline, photographed at Hammersmith Farm, Newport, as a debutante. She made her formal debut into Newport Society in the summer of 1947, just before her eighteenth birthday. In a conversation with the author, she implied that she didn't take being a debutante very seriously but went through the motions to please her mother.

Jacqueline and her friend Rose Grosvenor, before their joint coming-out dance at the Clambake Club in Newport, July 1947.

Jacqueline with her father in East Hampton, August 1947, shortly after her debut in Newport at the Auchincloss estate and a few days before her eighteenth birthday. Note the fine tailoring of Jack Bouvier's tan gabardine suit and Jacqueline's sudden maturity.

months later, on January 15, 1948. I remember asking Jacqueline about her debutante party in Newport and her dismissing my question with a remark like, "Oh, Jack, it was OK, very nice, all of Mummy's friends were there." It was obvious from her unenthusiastic tone that debutante parties meant little to her but very much to the socially ambitious Janet.

Jacqueline had learned to keep her two worlds totally apart. In Newport, she was in her mother's realm, where Janet had virtually welded her to the Auchinclosses. In East Hampton, she was in her father's domain: the Maidstone Club, Big Edie's Grey Gardens, family reunions at Lasata, and her greatest loves, her horses. Now a new life awaited her. She would soon be going to Vassar and taking her first trip to Europe.

Chapter Six

The Death
of Grampy Jack

*N*ot long after Jacqueline entered Vassar College in Pough-keepsie, New York, in the fall of 1947, an honor of sorts was bestowed on her that embarrassed more than it flattered her. Cholly Knickerbocker, the Hearst papers' syndicated gossip columnist and a self-styled social arbiter, a half-Russian, half-Italian, man-about-town whose real name was Igor Cassini, nominated her Debutante of the Year. The accolade first appeared in the *New York Journal American* and then in hundreds of Hearst papers throughout the nation:

> America is a country of traditions. Every four years we elect a president, every two years our congressmen. And every year a new Queen of Debutantes is crowned. . . . The Queen Deb of the year for 1947 is Jacqueline Bouvier, a regal brunette who has classic features and the daintiness of Dresden porcelain. She has poise, is softspoken and intelligent, everything the leading debutante should be. Her background is strictly "Old Guard." . . . Jacqueline is now studying at Vassar. You don't have to read a batch of press clippings to be aware of her qualities.

In those pre-television days, Cholly Knickerbocker's column was the equivalent of *The Tonight Show*. If you were prominently mentioned, you were guaranteed a measure of instant national fame. Now Jacqueline's fame, which was to reach gargantuan proportions sixteen years later, had spread beyond the horsey set of Long Island's East End to a wider, if still amorphous, audience.

The Cholly Knickerbocker nomination brought more annoyance than blessings. At nineteen, Jacqueline was sure enough of herself not to need an ego trip from a gossip columnist. Among other irritations, it distanced her from her freshman classmates at Vassar, earning her both their jealousy and their derision. Although she did very well in her studies, socially Jacqueline never was quite accepted by girls at Vassar, and, insofar as the boys were concerned, Cassini's anointing of her led chiefly to a series of disappointments.

I remember the dances in New York that winter—the assemblies, cotillions, and debutante balls—when the young blades from Princeton, Harvard, and Yale would come up to me in the stag line and ask, "Hey, what's wrong with that Debutante-of-the-Year cousin of yours? She doesn't put out. You can't even dance cheek-to-cheek with her." Or "What's the story on your Queen Deb cousin? You can't get even *halfway* to first base with her."

It was always the same with Jacqueline's admirers and would-be lovers. They all knew of her Debutante-of-the-Year status and wanted to make out with her, and she deflated all of them. Jacqueline did not just play hard to get—she was impossible to get. Her father had helped make her that way. He had written and admonished her many times not to forget that "all men are rats" and that it was "fatal" to make herself seem "available" or "easy." "Always keep them guessing," he would tell her.

Having Jacqueline named Debutante of the Year meant very little to Jack Bouvier, who had no use for Cholly Knickerbocker or any other gossip columnist since he had suffered considerably from them in the past, especially at the time of his divorce.

I don't believe Jacqueline herself took Cholly Knickerbocker's honor very seriously. When I raised the Queen Deb thing with her once, she told me she was much prouder of making the Dean's List during her first term at Vassar. Frankly, although Jacqueline was then a very striking looking and accomplished young woman, I think Cholly singled her out for the exotic aura of her name. Jacqueline Bouvier. Would the society columnist have bestowed the Queen Deb crown on a Joan Hall?

The futile advances of all those suitors occurred during the pre–sexual revolution fall–winter of 1947. The only man in Jacqueline's life in those days was pictured in a framed photograph she kept on her desk at Vassar: her father. All the girls who came into her room would gawk at it and swoon over her father's Hollywood looks.

Jacqueline was not particularly happy during her first year in Poughkeepsie, a provincial manufacturing town on the east bank of the Hudson, home of the Matthew Vassar Brewery and the Smith Brothers Cough Drop factory. "That goddamn Vassar" she would call it. Poughkeepsie bored her. There were few places to go for a drink or a snack, and the town's one decent clothing store, Peck and Peck, was beyond her means. In New York, she could charge clothes to Daddy at Saks and Bloomingdale's. Instead of hanging out with her classmates on weekends, she would take off for her father's New York apartment, or for football weekends at Yale and Princeton, or, God forbid, as far as Jack Bouvier was concerned, Merrywood.

Frequently, when she visited her father's apartment, Jacqueline would be surprised to find a young girl there—her fifty-eight-year-old father's newest flame. What would surprise her most would be her realization that her father's girlfriend was only a few years older than she was, perhaps twenty-one or twenty-two.

As December neared, Jack wrote his daughters that although Grandfather Bouvier was very ill with prostate cancer, he was expected to hold his traditional Christmas feast at his apartment at 765 Park Avenue. All the members of the Bouvier family would be present, including the Beale brothers and Michel Bouvier, who had all by then been mustered out of military service. To everyone's dismay, Grampy Jack took an abrupt turn for the worse in

Jacqueline kept this photo of her father prominently displayed in her room at Vassar, where her classmates would come in and swoon over it. The photo, which had also had a place of honor on her desk at Miss Porter's School, shows Jack Bouvier vacationing in Havana in the 1920s.

early December. On December 7 he wrote in his diary: "Lost all hope for improvement . . . walked in desperation ½ mile." Two weeks later, he confided to his diary that he felt "utterly miserable and incapable of the slightest exertion." He was now being taken care of by his maid of many years, Esther, and was soon joined by his forty-two-year-old divorced daughter, Michelle.

Three days before Christmas, Esther called up everybody and said there would be no traditional Christmas luncheon. The Major was feeling "profoundly depressed" and would have to miss Midnight Mass. The next day, Michelle arrived to take care of her father during what would be the last twenty days of his life.

On December 31, 1947, Grampy Jack went to bed and remained there, lying beneath the golden eagle Joseph Bonaparte had given his grandfather, until he died at 4 A.M. on January 15 at the age of eighty-three.

John Vernou Bouvier Jr. received the leading obituaries in both the *New York Herald Tribune* and the *New York Times,* which praised his patriotism, his oratorical skills, and his high place in New York's legal profession. His funeral in St. Patrick's drew a huge crowd of mourners. His remains were later driven to St. Philomena's cemetery in East Hampton, where he was finally laid to rest next to his mother, father, wife, and ill-fated son Bud.

The death of a patriarch of a large and prominent clan can be a cataclysmic event for a family. All of a sudden the center is gone, and there is no one to fill the void. Jack Bouvier was certainly in no position to assume the family leadership—he had neither the money nor the respect. Soon the "Black Orchid" would find himself generally ignored by his sisters, nieces, and nephews.

When Grandfather's will was read, it was clear that Jack had also been largely ignored by his father. They had never gotten along particularly well and had shared few interests.

Everyone in the family was shocked to learn how comparatively little Grampy Jack left to his heirs, considering what he had received from his forebears. In 1926, he inherited around $250,000, after taxes, from his father. Then, in 1935, in the depths of the depression, his bachelor uncle, M. C. Bouvier, had left an estate of

$3,227,997, of which he received $1,300,000 after taxes. And yet Grandfather Bouvier left only $824,000 to his hungry heirs and a voracious IRS—$726,000 less than he had received from his parents and uncle. Those treasured twenty-four years at Lasata, with its tennis court, riding ring, stables, gardens, fountains, statues, cornfields, orchards, vast lawns, four maids, cook, gardener, and chauffeur, and the charming six-bedroom Wildmoor, and the deluxe four-bedroom Park Avenue apartment had swallowed something in the neighborhood of three-quarters of a million dollars of his capital.

As it turned out, Jack received $100,000, free of taxes, and had a $50,000 loan excused; Edith received only $65,000 in trust; and his oldest grandchild, Bud's son, Michel Bouvier, got $28,000. The U.S. government took $210,000, New York State $15,000, and each of his nine other grandchildren received $3,000. The twins, Maude and Michelle, as the residuary legatees, divided the $237,000 that remained after all the bequests, taxes, and stocks, bonds, and real estate were sold.

During the highly contentious estate settlement, which involved a good deal of nasty wrangling among the legatees, Jack Bouvier evinced no interest in acquiring any of his late father's books, furnishings, family portraits, or papers, including those of the Founding Father and the Civil War letters of his grandfather. All Jack wanted from the estate was cash. Consequently, all the Bouvier portraits, heirlooms, photographs, and papers went to the twins and, ultimately, as a result of my mother's generosity, to the family biographer—me.

Apparently Jacqueline was very concerned about what her father was going to do with her $3,000 inheritance, for Jack wrote his two girls in February, in reply to their anxious queries, that he would not place the money in risky investments. "Stocks are not for young girls, or young women, or married women, or any kind of a woman," he told them. He intended to invest their money in U.S. Treasury bonds or place it in a savings account.

Living with the wealthy Auchinclosses and having to depend on her father for her paltry allowance of $50 a month made

Jacqueline feel very poor indeed. And now her much loved and admired grandfather, from whom we all expected to receive substantial legacies, had spent so much of his Bouvier patrimony that all he could leave us was a mere $3,000 apiece. I believe, beyond any doubt, that Jacqueline's penchant for marrying very rich men, and then spending their money extravagantly, ultimately derived from her feelings of relative poverty as a teenager. Here she was, living on vast estates with the Auchincloss children, Yusha, Nina Gore, and Tommy, who received much larger allowances. Her $50 a month was for everything—clothes, cosmetics, transportation. Why didn't she take a job on campus or in Poughkeepsie? The answer is that, in those days, it was unthinkable for a girl from her class to do *menial work* for pin money. Besides, that would make her feel even poorer.

Then there was her mother. Janet came from a family much richer than the Bouviers, although one would never suspect it from contact with the Lees in East Hampton. They lived in a modest house on Lily Pond Lane and Mr. Lee was very unassuming. We all knew he was reputed to be very rich, but none of us realized that he was worth $35 million. What we knew was that he was extremely parsimonious. Although he initially helped out with Jack and Janet's rent, he rarely gave Jacqueline or Lee a cent. And when Jacqueline married John F. Kennedy, Lee, an arch Republican who hated Kennedy's father, disinherited Jacqueline and Lee entirely and refused to come to Kennedy's inauguration. He died in 1968 without having seen his famous granddaughter in fifteen years.

Yes, Jacqueline felt very poor as a teenager, but her mother had taught her a way out. Wasn't Janet eking out just a spare existence on Jack Bouvier's alimony of $1,050 a month when, in the second year of her life as a neurotic divorcée, along came Hugh D. Auchincloss Jr., who, in one stroke, lifted her up to be the mistress of two enormous estates, provided her with all the money she wanted, and fathered two charming children with her.

The lesson was obvious. The answer to money problems was to marry a rich man. Janet would make this very clear when some years later, Jacqueline fell for a young stockbroker, John G. W. Husted Jr., the son of a prominent New York banker who was a Yale graduate and whose parents knew both the Bouviers and the Auchinclosses. The romance lasted about four months and culminated in young Husted's presenting Jacqueline with a diamond and sapphire engagement ring that once belonged to his mother. Then Janet asked Husted how much money he was making on Wall Street. When she learned the answer was $17,000 a year, she called off the marriage. Jack Bouvier earned around $45,000 annually when Janet married him; Hughdie was making hundreds of thousands. John G. W. Husted Jr., for all his fine qualities, wasn't rich enough—that was all there was to it. Janet was out for far bigger game for Jacqueline and she let her daughter know it.

Jacqueline's response to her mother's advice, and also, to some extent, her father's, was to do no more than occasionally flirt with a man she liked, then, as soon as she discovered he had no money, no *big* money, to drop him like the proverbial hot potato.

Jacqueline returned to Vassar after her grandfather's funeral fully realizing that things in the Bouvier family had changed dramatically. Her twin aunts, as the residuary legatees of their father's estate, had inherited Lasata and decided to sell it as soon as they could find an acceptable buyer. This meant she could not go to East Hampton in August, for what was East Hampton without Lasata?

Accordingly, she began making plans for a trip to Europe in July and August with two of her Vassar classmates, Helen and Judy Bowdin, the stepdaughters of Edward F. Foley, Undersecretary of the Treasury, and Julia Bissell of Wilmington. Helen Shearman, Jacqueline's former teacher at Holton-Arms in Washington, agreed to chaperone, since in those days nice young girls were not allowed to travel abroad on their own.

Meanwhile, Jacqueline did well in her courses and received high grades in Florence Lowell's history of religion course and Helen Sandison's Shakespeare course, which Jacqueline claimed gave her a lifelong love of the Bard's poetry and plays.

And she continued her often contentious correspondence with her father. In response to a letter in which Jacqueline had written that she was embarrassed by what two boys had told her about her father taking out their mothers long ago, Jack remonstrated that she should realize he wouldn't have taken them out unless they were very attractive and that she should feel proud, not irritated, that he dated them and that they remembered him after all these years.

In May, Jack wrote several argumentative letters to Jacqueline in which he observed that he knew she had scarcely any money in the bank, but he might send her a check if she didn't neglect him so much and would recognize that he was still her father and naturally interested in her and all she did.

In another May letter, Jack expressed his surprise and annoyance over being told at the last minute of Jacqueline's plans to spend the summer traveling in Europe. He was particularly annoyed because he had already made all his plans, which, of course, included a visit from Jackie. He was suspicious that Janet was happy about the trip because it would take place during the time Jacqueline was supposed to be visiting him in East Hampton, and Janet always was delighted when she could keep Jackie away from him.

He suspected that when Jacqueline returned on August 25 she would want to go to Newport and stay at Hammersmith Farm until after Labor Day. He insisted that she visit him in East Hampton for a week before she returned to Vassar, and warned that if she didn't visit him, he could cut off her allowance for good and not give her any spending money for Europe.

Before Jacqueline departed on her European tour, there was a flurry of correspondence between Jack and his girls. Some of it was amusing, some admonitory. One of the more lighthearted letters centered on his current girlfriend, Sally Butler, a beautiful Pan-American Airlines employee stationed in Miami who was not much older than Jacqueline. Jack wrote his daughter to stop picking on Sally. "I would much rather have Sally than any of those old bags in Newport . . . who are supposed to represent society." He then admitted that while Sally was too young for him, she was fun to be with; even though she did not belong to society, as such, her father was a doctor, and she spoke Spanish perfectly and had graduated from the University of North Carolina.

Before leaving, Jacqueline ran up a $201.58 bill at Bloomingdale's for a set of made-to-order draperies for her father's apartment without obtaining his permission. When Jack received the bill, he told his other daughter, Lee, that he believed Jacqueline came to his apartment not to see him, but only to redecorate the place. Accordingly, he canceled the order and told Jacqueline that although he admitted his apartment was rather drab—it was furnished with worn-out or discarded tables, chairs, and dressers from the attic at Lasata—there would be no more unauthorized redecorating.

Jacqueline had a mania for redecorating, and would not give up her attempts to transform her father's staid, musty bachelor's quarters into something out of *Vogue* or *House and Garden,* but that would have to wait for her return from Europe.

On July 9, Jacqueline, her three Vassar classmates, and their chaperone set sail for England aboard the *Queen Mary* for what turned out to be, in Judy Bowdin's words, "the most grueling and tightly scheduled seven weeks I have ever spent. Every minute was accounted for."

The trip's high point was a royal garden party at Buckingham Palace that Undersecretary Foley had arranged for his stepdaughters and Jacqueline months in advance. For the event, the girls had packed dressy new white chiffon afternoon gowns, wide-brimmed straw hats, and elbow-length white gloves.

Unfortunately, the party had to be held under tents in a driving summer rain. Jacqueline and her friends curtsied to King

George VI and Queen Elizabeth in a packed tent crammed with refreshment tables. Sir Winston Churchill, seventy-four, and destined to be Prime Minister again in 1951, was in attendance. Jacqueline was so impressed by him that she went through the receiving line twice to shake hands with the hero of World War II.

After a breathless tour of London and southern England, the quartet sailed to LeHavre to savor Paris and the chateaux of the Loire Valley, followed by a visit to Juan les Pins on the French Riviera. There they bumped into Churchill again, this time as he was painting a seascape.

After a day and night in Juan les Pins, they set off on an exhausting tour of Switzerland and Italy, stopping at Lucerne, Zurich, Interlaken, the Jungfrau, Milan, Venice, Verona, Florence, and Rome.

While Jacqueline was racing through Europe, Jack Bouvier wrote her a long, newsy letter telling her that Lee had just completed a nine-day stay with him at a charming cottage he had rented off the Montauk highway and warning that she would have to look more beautiful than ever or else her younger sister would steal a lot of her boyfriends.

Jack wrote his favorite daughter that he was fed up with both her and Lee, and would no longer bother to make plans for having either of them with him during the summer. It's too absurd, he whined; it's clear that you now prefer Newport to East Hampton.

But then he softened and told Jackie that he couldn't wait to see her. Since he would be working on Wall Street when her ship arrived in New York, he invited her to come up to his apartment after she had greeted all the Auchinclosses at the pier.

Although the pace of her trip to Europe was hectic, Jacqueline vowed to return for a more leisurely stay so she could really absorb the culture of the old world. Before that opportunity, however, another year at Vassar loomed before her, as well as another year of bitter wrangling with her parents over who would enjoy her company on weekends, holidays, and summer vacations.

Chapter Seven

Vassar and the Sorbonne

$\mathcal{A}$ s her father had predicted, Jacqueline was greeted by a contingent of Auchinclosses at the pier on her return from Europe, but, as promised, she left them for Jack Bouvier's apartment. Jack was delighted to see the light—and torment—of his life, and the two spent a happy three days together before Jacqueline went up to Hammersmith Farm to get ready for her sophomore year at Vassar.

Jacqueline was soon back in her college routine, studying hard all week and taking off weekends for Yale and Princeton, and occasionally her father's apartment, to keep him from complaining that she neglected him and make sure he would not carry out his periodic threats to cut off her monthly allowance.

Not long after her return to Vassar, she spotted a notice on a bulletin board advertising the Smith College Junior Year Abroad Program. Intrigued, Jacqueline sought out the Dean of the College for advice and was soon applying for admission to the program. She expressed her desire to spend her junior year in Paris attending the Sorbonne, a college founded in 1250, which was joined by Napoleon to the University of Paris in 1808, and specialized in teaching French civilization to foreign students.

By then Jacqueline had matured intellectually and spiritually to a considerable degree since entering Vassar as a freshman. A classmate from her sophomore year, Joan Ellis Ferguson, wrote a tribute to Jacqueline in the *Vassar Alumnae Quarterly* after Jacqueline's death in May 1994:

> After a particularly contentious philosophy class devoted to authoritarianism, I returned to Main in a state of irritation at the rigidity of the Catholic Church. Who, I demanded of a friend, with all the uninformed intensity of a seventeen-year-old, could possibly explain and defend this tyranny to me? "Talk to Jackie after dinner" came the answer. We sat on the floor in the Main North Parlor while she roamed wonderfully through the fields of philosophy, religion, and history, and quietly talked about her faith. I remember thinking: "she is reading things I haven't even heard of."

Whether Jacqueline, by her sophomore year, had "found religion" is open to question. Like me, and the rest of her Bouvier cousins, Jacqueline seemed then not to take the Catholic faith, in which we were all brought up, very seriously. But I do remember being struck by her intense interest in art and literature at that time. I was a Princeton sophomore when Jacqueline was a sophomore at Vassar, and occasionally she would visit for a football weekend. We would discuss the courses we were taking and I could tell she was undergoing somewhat of an intellectual awakening, as I too was. She certainly no longer gave the impression of being exclusively preoccupied with the care and feeding of horses.

Several of her Vassar classmates have testified to this process of maturation, as well as to other facets of her personality. Harriet de Rossiére remembers Jackie striding into the Main Dining Hall in full riding habit—tweed jacket, white sweater, jodhpurs, and boots—and immediately cracking jokes about the food. "She had a great sense of humor," Harriet observed. "But she was very secretive; you never knew what she was thinking or what she was really feeling." Harriet also remarked, "I know that she absolutely worshipped her father, who was considered a bit of a rake," and that Jackie "effortlessly received the highest grades in the history of art." Years later, the journalist Charlotte Curtis, also a classmate, told Harriet that she once saw Jackie "flush an armful of Jack Kennedy's letters down the drain."

Another classmate, Joan Kupfer Ross, remembers, with affection, the help in her courses Jackie gave when Joan was ill for an entire term in the Vassar infirmary. She particularly recalls the notes Jackie brought to her from the history lectures she missed. "The notes took my breath away," she told me. "They were a very model of beautiful penmanship, organization, clarity, and completeness. They made the complex simple. They were devoid of fat. Lean, clear, and filled with implicit understanding, they made it easy for me to know the content of the course and as a result I did well on the final exam. I missed her presence very much when she left for Paris to attend the Sorbonne. Years later I remembered the clarity of those notes and in the long years since then felt that I could discern those same qualities appearing in the public decisions she made as First Lady and thereafter."

Meanwhile, Jacqueline was inundated with a steady stream of advice from her father about how she should behave with men. Apparently, she had dropped all her plans one weekend in order to rush up to New Haven for a date with a handsome Yalie whom she hardly knew. Jack Bouvier had gotten the impression, rightly or wrongly, that she just couldn't wait to be in his arms.

Concerned that Jacqueline would harm her reputation, he told her very emphatically that it was a very unwise thing to give a young man the sense that she was utterly delighted to take a trip to see him, no matter who he was. He could be the president of his class or the head of Skull and Bones, for all he cared. By acting so overjoyed to receive the invitation, she would only be showing her own lack of self-respect and giving the young man's friends the idea of how easy it would be to entice her to New Haven. He told her not to forget that for years he had advised her always to play hard to get.

Evidently, the Yalie almost let Jacqueline get stranded in New Haven, where she would be at his mercy, and she was compelled to take two late-night train rides by herself. Jack told his daughter angrily that the boy in question "ought to be shot" for forcing an eighteen-year-old girl to take the 9:30 P.M. train from New Haven to New York and then the 12:00 A.M. train from New York to Poughkeepsie. No boy is good enough, he admonished her, for her to take a lengthy trip like that alone at that late hour.

Jack also scolded his daughter for even considering visiting a boy's apartment alone. That had not been considered proper in his day and, he persisted, still was not. Never give a boy the impression you are easy, he counseled, and remember: "All men are rats"—don't give any of them a chance to take a nip out of you.

Jack's concern for propriety also extended to Jacqueline's relationship with Yusha Auchincloss, whom she had referred to in a letter as her "stepbrother." Jack forbade Jacqueline to take a car trip out West with him. Jack told her that he would not allow her or Lee to take *any* long motor trips unless there was an older person along. He added, "I don't give a damn if you think Yusha is your step-brother or not. He definitely is *not* a step-brother, but if you choose to call him that you should insert the words 'by marriage.'"

Jacqueline must have wearied of her father's relentless harangues, especially about her spending habits. On one occasion Jack berated his eldest daughter for spending too much money. He had just paid a bill for $24 for her cosmetics and another for $20 for photos taken at her cousin Shella's party, and had given her $20 to see Lee. If she would be more thoughtful and stop charging so many of her expenses to him, she would get her allowance of $50 a month on time, he told her. On another occasion, he would complain bitterly of all the purchases she charged to him at Bloomingdale's and Saks, as much as $36 worth.

This was to be a habit she could never shake. John F. Kennedy was aghast when she spent the equivalent of his entire salary as president—$100,000—on clothes alone. To which Jacqueline would counter: "I have to dress well, Jack, so I won't embarrass you. As a public figure you'd be humiliated if I was photographed in some saggy old housedress. Everyone would say your wife is a slob and refuse to vote for you." Years later, Aristotle Onassis became furious at her for charging hundreds of thousands of dollars' worth of clothing, jewelry, and sundries to Olympic Airways.

Jacqueline could really drive her father crazy when she used money that he had sent her to visit him in New York for traveling to see the hated Auchinclosses at Merrywood instead. It all boils down to her being too selfish, he wrote. She had to start denying herself things she wanted now, because as she got older she would find self-denial increasingly difficult. She can't expect to have her every wish fulfilled, he advised, while pointing out that character is developed through renunciation.

Jack continued in the same vein, telling her that, although she resembled him in many ways, she was getting to be more and more like her mother. As an example of this inherited lack of generosity, he mentioned Jackie's reactions when they had discussed some of the bequests he planned to put into his will. Jacqueline had objected to one, saying, "I don't see why she should get anything." He adamantly advised her not to emulate her mother, reminding her of Janet's want of generosity and repeating what he had told her many times—that Janet had been nothing but a gold digger all her life.

The trouble, of course, was that Jacqueline at nineteen was a beautiful, talented, intelligent, and energetic young woman eager to live life to the hilt. Her father, who was now almost sixty, was desperately trying to hold on to her and her sister, the only people, who gave meaning to his life. He now had this terribly formidable enemy to contend with: Janet and the Auchincloss brood, which seemed to him like a small, hostile army.

In early March 1949, Jacqueline received word that she had been accepted in the Smith program and immediately notified her father. He wrote back that he was, of course, very proud, observing that he knew that whenever she was determined to get something she wanted she usually did. He also told her that they should go out on the town more often together because they always had fun, always found mutually interesting things to talk about, and unfailingly made a big impression on people, always attracting admiring glances wherever they went. Jack was absolutely correct in this observation. He and Jacqueline made a stunning couple, and he was very vain about it. He loved showing her off at all his Manhattan haunts.

Yet despite his obvious pride in his daughter, he lectured her again and again about what he considered her selfishness, telling her that when she wanted something, she just kept insisting and insisting and insisting until she had gotten it. Was Jack being fair to his daughter with this relentless criticism? To some extent, no. He had become the underdog in his long battle for her affection and he took out his frustration on her.

Now that Jacqueline knew she was going to the Sorbonne, she realized that she did not want to return to Vassar after her year abroad; she was "fed up with Vassar." She had never adjusted to college campus life and had fled every weekend for New York, Washington, or some Ivy League college. The Vassar girls had retaliated by refusing to admit her to the Daisy Chain, an honor equivalent to being tapped for a prestigious sorority. The rejection was a blow to Jacqueline's pride, so she had decided not to spend her senior year in Poughkeepsie. She was toying with the idea of becoming a photographer's model. Jack was predictably averse to this, telling her "you don't waste a college education and a year at the Sorbonne to be a model in New York City—so forget that particular idea."

However, he wouldn't mind her coming to live with him in New York, informing her that he was contemplating taking her into his brokerage firm after she turned twenty-one in July 1950. His idea was to have her live with him from September 1950 to June 1951, and work in his office, on a part-time basis, for $50 a week, more money than she ever had.

"I'm not begging you to come by any means," he told her, but, if she preferred to stay in Virginia and ride "those plugs," she shouldn't expect him ever to invite her again, "certainly not in the near future." Jack was, of course, anxious about her choosing the Auchinclosses over him when she returned from her studies at the Sorbonne.

I had a chance to experience the Auchincloss world firsthand that summer of 1949 when I was a cadet at the U.S. Navy Reserve Officer's Candidate School in Newport. The naval base where I lived and trained was not far from Hammersmith Farm, so I would spend my one twenty-four-hour liberty each week there, or at the Newport Country Club, or at Bailey's Beach, as a guest of the Auchinclosses. I will admit that I forced myself on them to a certain extent, justifying my intrusiveness by the fact that, after all, Aunt Janet *was* my godmother and I had never felt divorced from her or Jackie, whom I continued to love very much. I learned from Janet that she felt things had changed between us significantly, and that she thought Uncle Jack may have sent me to spy on her and Jackie.

Hammersmith Farm stood on a grassy hill overlooking Narragansett Bay. It had views of lawn and pastures and farm buildings on one side, and a garden designed by Frederick Law Olmstead, the creator of New York's Central Park, on the other. Hughdie had inherited the seventy-eight-acre estate from his mother, who had it built in 1887 at some remove from the great Vanderbilt Palaces—The Breakers and Marble House—that line Bellevue Avenue below, because she did not want to appear as ostentatious about her family's wealth as the Vanderbilts were about theirs and wished to project a different identity.

The main house was a large, barnlike Victorian structure whose multi-tiered roof sprouted many gables, cupolas, and chimneys. My first impression was that it looked spooky. Inside were twenty-eight dark rooms, some of them huge, and thirteen fireplaces. Sixteen servants looked after the Auchinclosses in this House That Standard Oil Had Built.

My first impression of the mansion as a cadet in officers training was of its vast gloom: large, drafty rooms filled with heavy, dark, Victorian furniture and great stuffed heads of bear, moose, and reindeer staring down from the walls.

What a difference from Lasata, I mused. The French-Italian influence was completely absent. No sunken Italian gardens, their radiance framed by dark hawthorn hedges, no carved sundial, no

Hammersmith Farm, residence of Hugh D. Auchincloss Jr., in Newport, Rhode Island. Jacqueline lived here part of every summer from 1942 until September 12, 1953, when she married Senator John F. Kennedy. The wedding reception took place on the property. In 1974, Hammersmith Farm was sold to a group of businessmen who turned it into a museum called Camelot Gardens.

mossy fountain, no graceful French shepherdesses. Just a vast green lawn and meadow, then this enormous building that reminded me of a stark Jesuit novitiate I had once visited outside Philadelphia.

How was Jacqueline surviving in this hilltop gloom? Soon I was ushered upstairs to the huge Deck Room where she and Janet were waiting. Knowing how Uncle Jack felt about the Auchinclosses, I felt I was in an enemy camp, and had the feeling from the assembled Auchinclosses that they too sensed they had somehow let the opposition in. Here was Jacqueline, surrounded by her tall, rigid, uncommunicative stepfather, her now stiff, ultraformal mother, and assorted Auchincloss stepchildren, and looking uncustomarily stiff and nervous herself, and decidedly trapped. I wanted to run up and kiss her, as I normally would have, but, before I

John H. Davis as a naval officer stationed in Newport when he visited Jacqueline, who was staying with the Auchinclosses at Hammersmith Farm.

could, Aunt Janet guided me to an overstuffed brown leather chair and had one of the maids bring me a tall glass of iced tea. Jacqueline followed and sat down opposite on a long brown leather sofa, with Janet leaning on one of its enormous arms.

I was bursting to ask Jacqueline how she was getting along with the Auchinclosses, how she liked Hammersmith Farm, and tell her of the virtual dismantling of Lasata and how much Uncle Jack missed her and Lee, but I couldn't say a word. Janet was perched on that sofa arm like a falcon who could see and hear everything. And so Jacqueline and I were compelled to bypass the Bouvier-Auchincloss feud and simply discuss our own upcoming adventures: how exciting it was that Jacqueline would soon be at the Sorbonne and I would be a naval officer attached to a ship with the Atlantic Fleet. After telling me that she first would have to take an intensive course in French at the University of Grenoble beginning in mid-August, Jacqueline said, in that very polite, whispery voice of hers, that I and my friends, Ralph Peters and Don Scott (two Princeton roommates also training at Newport that summer), were welcome to use the Auchincloss cabana at Bailey's Beach and sign the Auchincloss name at the Golf Club. After I offered my profuse thanks, Janet and Jacqueline ushered me through the immense spaces of Hammersmith and out under the portico, where we said good-bye.

I visited Jacqueline and Janet and Hughdie and Yusha and all the other Auchinclosses every weekend for the duration of my naval training that summer. But in my fleeting conversations with Jacqueline, mostly held at Bailey's Beach, there always was an Auchincloss listening in. Thus, the Bouvier spy would have no ammunition to bring back to Uncle Jack.

Just before Jacqueline was due to set sail for France, she did agree to spend some time with her father in East Hampton. Black Jack had written that he would again play the "Sucker," so far as she was concerned, and would go to East Hampton for the last two weeks of July. He made it perfectly clear, however, that he would not relish passing the Lee cabana at the Maidstone Club with the Lees watching his every move. He would do it for his

Jacqueline models at an East Hampton fashion show in August 1949. Her fellow model is her friend Elizabeth "Liz" Fly, who is now married to the noted New York financier Felix Rohatyn. At twenty Jacqueline is now taking an interest in clothes that she hadn't shown during her childhood and teenage years. In time, clothes would become an all-consuming passion. By the time she reached the White House, she was spending $100,000 a year on clothes alone.

darling daughter, whom he so loved. I was still in training at Newport when Jacqueline went down to East Hampton to be with her father and her horses for the last time before heading off for France. I remember saying "au revoir" to her at Bailey's Beach the day before she left. "Oh Jack," she gushed, "I'm so excited about France. I can hardly *wait* to go!"

With Lasata closed so that real estate agents could show it to prospective buyers, the Bouviers were staying at Wildmoor, and that is where I believe Jacqueline's twentieth birthday party was celebrated on July 28. Big Edie apparently gave her a great send-off, belting out both French and American songs, and concluding with a rousing rendition of "La Marseillaise."

Jacqueline sailed for France on August 24. About ten days later, she was in the medieval town of Grenoble at the foot of the French Alps boarding with a local family and attending intensive courses in the French language and French literature where it was forbidden to speak any language other than French. As soon as she got settled, she wrote her father, reassuring him that her lower back pain had almost gone away—she had suffered a slipped disc while riding Danseuse in East Hampton, perhaps for the last time.

Jacqueline had also written that she planned to take a trip to Corsica to see the birthplace of Napoleon and his brothers and sisters. She had been made well aware by Grampy Jack that her great-great-grandfather had fought for Napoleon at Waterloo, and that his eldest brother, Joseph Bonaparte, had helped him to get a start in America.

Jack Bouvier was not too enthusiastic about this idea. Corsica, a large island between Italy and France that had been Italian, specifically Genoese, throughout most of its history, and where Italian had been, and still was, the main spoken language, had a reputation as a wild, out-of-the-way place teeming with fierce brigands and French mafiosi. For this reason, Jack counseled Jacqueline against going there, peppering his warning with more advice on how to behave with men. He told her not to go unless Marie Andre, the French girl she was living with, accompanied her. He informed Jackie that he himself had found Corsica "quite a tough place" on his visit there. He conceded that she probably thought he was old-fashioned, but insisted he wasn't—his warnings were based on his own experience. He was just the opposite and wrote that "no one knows the low-down of life and the sexes better than I do."

Jacqueline did heed her father's advice and refrained from going to Corsica, much to his relief. He wrote again, urging her to find someplace on the Italian Riviera where she could do some swimming and get plenty of sun to help heal her back.

Jacqueline pleased her father when she wrote him that if business on Wall Street was bad, he shouldn't send her an increase in her allowance. He told her that this was one of the most generous offers she had made in many years because it showed that she was not just thinking of herself.

During her stay at Grenoble, Jacqueline and groups of students would take side trips in southern France, or *le Midi,* as the French call it. One of these trips took her to the towns of the nearby Rhône Valley—Valence, Nîmes, and Arles—where distant cousins of hers lived whose existence she was unaware of at the time. I discovered them later while researching my book *The Bouviers* in 1967.

She described the experience of descending from mountainous Grenoble to the plains of Provence to one of her first biographers, Mary Van Rensselaer Thayer. I had the same experience myself when I was researching my book. You descend from the cold rugged, mountainous terrain of Grenoble, where the dominant color is a slate gray, to suddenly behold this wide, radiant plain vibrating with bright colors—yellow, orange, scarlet—under a clear blue sky. Soon you are driving along narrow country roads bordered by rows of poplars, which also range out into the fields to protect the crops from the destructive mistral, a harsh wind that blows in from the Mediterranean. It is a happy, bucolic landscape peopled largely by descendants of farmers who have tilled this rich earth since Roman times. These simple, happy people speak French with the curious "accent du Midi," which often confounds Frenchmen from the northern provinces. Jacqueline was eager to visit the Camargue, a broad stretch of the Rhone delta which is flooded by the river and the

Mediterranean once a year and where the young people of the area wade into the flood on horses and bless it in a ceremony they call "la Bénédiction de la Mer." Another colorful feature of this region is the gypsy population, who can be seen tending wild horses and bulls.

This was the land of Jacqueline's ancestors—Provence—although she did not realize it because of the distortions Grandfather Bouvier had made about his ancestry in his family history *Our Forebears*. When Jacqueline took her foray into the land Julius Caesar had conquered, she did not know that a family of her "petites cousines" lived about a half-mile from the magnificent Triumphal Arch built to commemorate his victories in what is today known as Orange. And she had a cousin of about her age, who, in the fall, after making wine, would ride wild horses in the Camargue.

Toward the end of her stay in Grenoble, just before she journeyed back to Paris, Jacqueline took a short trip to southern Italy. She drove along the spectacular Amalfi Coast, stopping for a moment at the medieval hilltop village of Ravello, which she would visit twelve years later as First Lady in the company of her sister Lee and Lee's new husband, Prince Stanislaus Radziwill.

In one of his letters, Jack urged Jacqueline to write him more regularly, expressed contentment that her back was better, and told her what a delightful visit he recently had with Lee. But there was never any question about which daughter's company he preferred. He conceded in another letter that Jackie was his favorite daughter: "You have all my love, Darling, and although we are separated by three thousand miles, still I think my love for you is greater perhaps than when you were here with me at 125 East 74th Street."

After her trip to Southern Italy, Jacqueline settled into her new Paris home, a spacious apartment at 78 Avenue Mozart in the 12th arrondissement that belonged to Countess Guyot de Renty, a widow whose husband had served with her in the French Resistance, was captured by the Germans along with her, and ultimately died in a German concentration camp.

Besides the Countess, there was her daughter Claude, who was about Jacqueline's age, and her divorced daughter Ghislaine and Ghislaine's four-year-old son, Christian. Two other American girls boarded with the Countess, making seven guests in all. The Countess did all the cooking. There was no central heating and just one bathroom, which contained an antique tin bathtub. Only French was spoken in the Countess's household, which is the way Jacqueline had wanted it. She could have stayed at Reid Hall at the Sorbonne with the other American students, but she chose to live a strictly French existence. In this atmosphere Jacqueline blossomed, telling friends and family it was the happiest and most carefree year of her life.

When she wasn't attending lectures at the Sorbonne or studying in bed under piles of quilts and sweaters, Jacqueline was out seeing the sights and enjoying the myriad pleasures of Paris. She adored wandering through the Louvre and the gardens of Les Tuilleries, but she couldn't help indulging in her favorite sport, riding, which she had promised her father she wouldn't do because of her bad back. She made the mistake of writing her father that she had ridden a horse in the Bois du Boulogne, and on December 19 he fired off a letter, scolding her for breaking her word. He told her he was perusing the Smith bill at his desk when her letter was delivered and had impulsively decided to tear the bill up but didn't. He reminded her that they had made a compact that she would not ride until she returned home and now she had broken her agreement. Do not ride again, he admonished her. If she did, he might be forced to do something drastic.

Jacqueline herself did not have a lonely Christmas. She went to England during Christmas break and looked up someone she had grown quite close to eight years before—Anne Plugge, Jack's former wartime sweetheart. Jacqueline learned that Anne had given birth to twins shortly after returning to England with her husband; she had always wondered whether the twins were from her father or Colonel Plugge. And she was well aware that twins ran in the Bouvier family.

Jacqueline's curiosity must have been running high as she approached the Plugge cottage in a London suburb. Then, when Anne introduced the twins—a boy and a girl—Jacqueline's heart must have raced. Yes, they were undoubtedly Jack's. The boy looked just like him and the girl resembled her. The same broad faces. The same wide-apart eyes. The same hair and complexion. And they both had the prominent Bouvier chin. There was no question: Anne Plugge's twins were Bouviers.

We have no idea what passed between Jacqueline and Anne Plugge once Jacqueline came to this realization. Nor do we know what sort of a Christmas Colonel and Mrs. Plugge and their twins and Jacqueline celebrated on December 25, 1949. Knowing Jacqueline's love of children and her ability to demonstrate that love, we can assume that they all enjoyed a very merry time.

We also don't know what Jacqueline wrote her father about her visit with the Plugge family and her discovery of the Plugge twins' true paternity, but we do have Jack's reply to a question she asked. In a long letter of January 10, 1950, Jack put it bluntly: "You are dead right about the Plugge twins. They definitely could not be his, and there is no question about it."

The Plugge twins were a terrible secret to have to keep for the rest of one's life—her own half-brother and half-sister living in England under the name of Plugge. As it turned out, the Plugge twins met a tragic destiny. Both died in their twenties—the boy in an automobile accident in Morocco, the girl from a gunshot wound in Trinidad.

Enough said. Jack went on to speculate on what Jacqueline should do next. He encouraged her to write a book about her travels in Europe when she returned home, expressing confidence that it would be a best-seller.

Jack feared that while Jacqueline was abroad, she might develop such a love for Europe that she would not want to return home. He advised her that she might hate the thought of going back to "that damn Vassar" but assured her that graduating from Vassar would be a far bigger achievement than having spent her junior year at the Sorbonne.

Another continuing concern that weighed on his mind was the pull of the Auchinclosses. He had heard that her "dear mama" and "Toot Toot Tootsie" (Hugh D. Auchincloss Jr.) were sailing for Europe on January 20. He fervently hoped they would not interfere with her studies, although he was sure Janet would attempt to interfere because, after long experience, he knew she thrived on interfering.

When Jacqueline returned to Paris from England, she threw herself into a life that was part academic, part bohemian, and part being occasionally, as she phrased it in a letter to her father, "swanky." There were her studies at the Sorbonne, which she took very seriously, her ventures to the Left Bank cafés such as La Coupole, the Dome, and the Deux Magots, where Jean Paul Sartre and Simone de Beauvoir used to hold court, and her "swanky" excursions to the Ritz, for which she got all dressed and made up, wore her one fur coat, and hung out at the Ritz Bar with wealthy, sometimes titled French types and American expatriates.

Meanwhile Jack Bouvier kept up his steady barrage of letters, complained about Jacqueline's not writing him often enough, threatened to cut off her allowance if she continued to ignore him, and not so subtly tried to make her jealous of Lee, with whom he had been spending much time.

Occasionally Jack would unintentionally reveal that he felt sorry for himself. When he learned that Jacqueline planned to spend Easter vacation in Spain with a "friend," he wrote her that he had been thinking of visiting her at Easter, but "now . . . I would be going around by myself."

He never ceased to give his eldest daughter advice on how to behave with men. She had written him that she had a glamorous new beau who was on the staff of Premier Bidault. This elicited Jack's observation that a man who is an attaché, a diplomat in effect, is usually more suave and polished, and probably has a smoother line than other Frenchmen who are merely businessmen. He expressed a strong concern over this romance because he believed that she was too young to get tied down, and reminded her that she had a lot of hard work ahead. There are probably many more American attachés just as attractive, and he urged her to take her time about getting deeply involved. Wait until she was twenty-three, he told her, then she could do what she wanted. This, he emphasized, was a bargain between them: at twenty-three she could get married—provided, of course, he approved of the man.

That spring, Jacqueline's eccentric Aunt Edith had suffered a bad fire at her East Hampton house, and Jack asked Jacqueline to write her a letter of sympathy. Jack then showed the compassionate side of his nature when he told his daughter that it was wonderfully fulfilling to give a moment of pleasure to people who have a miserable, routine life trying to keep a house from falling down on their heads. If she wrote her Aunt Edie, he said, she would be "bringing much happiness" to an aunt who had a special love for her.

In April, a sad event occurred for the Bouvier family. Lasata was sold, and the great house and grounds that had been the family's focal point for the past twenty-five years was emptied of its contents. At the time the estate was sold—April 1950—the real estate market in East Hampton had gone sour, mainly due to the extraordinarily high cost of upkeep of such large properties and the unreasonably high property taxes. It took a full-time gardener and two laborers to maintain Lasata's elaborate and extensive flower and vegetable gardens, and the cornfields, lawns, clay tennis court, stables, and riding ring. Consequently, the estate was sold for only $40,000. The astute buyer was Page Hufty, a millionaire businessman from Washington and Palm Beach. Today the estate would bring in at least $10 million.

It fell to my mother and me to oversee the emptying of the house and its consignment to the new owner's agent. It was a damp, misty April morning when Mother and I arrived at the estate in the family station wagon to collect all the Bouvier papers, portraits, photographs, and memorabilia from the attic and from grandfather's studio and library. For some reason, Jack Bouvier, who, to his father's dismay, had never taken any interest in the family's history, had tagged these items for destruction.

We were met in front of the house by the vans that were to transport most of the furniture to Wildmoor, the smaller house on Appaquoque Road, three miles away, which had not yet been sold.

It was not until we entered the house and saw the movers carrying out the furniture that Mother and I felt the full emotional impact of what we were losing. At one point, we wandered out onto the brick terrace for a last look at the once elaborately manicured Italian garden. Two years of neglect had caused the hedges to grow so high that they overwhelmed the flowers that were just coming into bloom. The baroque fountain was silent and shrouded in moss and ivy, and we could just barely make out the statues of the French shepherdesses, so high had the bushes around them grown.

It was time to pack up and go. I climbed up to the attic and managed to save most of the family papers and photographs, including Louise Vernou's Civil War letters to her son, the wounded veteran of Gettysburg, most of M. C. Bouvier's business papers, and Grandfather's meticulously written diaries, in which he had faithfully recorded every event of every day of his adult life, and which have provided a guide to many of the events in this book.

In succeeding years, visits to Lasata by members of the Bouvier family have become increasingly painful as we have noted unwelcome changes in its buildings and a deterioration of its grounds. Two years ago, I drove through the back of the property that borders Middle Lane and was dismayed to find Jackie's riding ring in a state of collapse and overgrown by thistles, poison ivy, and other weeds. Then I glanced toward the stables and my heart sank as I beheld what had become a row of shanties—one roofless, another buckling at door level, another reduced to a pile of lumber and shingles. For an instant, I had a vision of a sunny August morning with Jacqueline prancing around the gleaming, white-fenced ring on Danseuse and perky Aunt Janet in her formal riding habit about to mount her chestnut mare Pas d'Or. Then there was life and action and beauty at Lasata's riding ring and stables; now there was a deathly shambles. No one had bothered to maintain the site of a great First Lady's childhood delights.

The sale of Lasata and the passing of its owner of twenty-five years marked the end of an era for the Bouviers. No one in the family was destined to live such a gracious and financially secure life again, except Jacqueline. Normally, the eldest male of a wealthy and prominent family inherits the money and property to carry on the family's lifestyle and traditions. But cousin Michel Bouvier had inherited only $28,000, and the other males, myself included, received only $3,000 apiece. Although I never discussed it with Jacqueline, I believe that she was fully aware of the decline of the Bouvier family's fortunes and that her pursuit of two very wealthy husbands was somehow related to that awareness. No, she was not going to be reduced to the pathetic condition of her father and the misery and squalor of her hermit-like Aunt Edith. Although she was genuinely attracted to John F. Kennedy, and came to love him, I believe she was also subliminally drawn to his family's wealth.

Shortly after the sale of Lasata, Janet and Hughdie showed up in Paris and took Jacqueline on a tour of Austria and Germany. They visited Vienna, Salzburg, Hitler's mountain retreat at Berchtesgaden, Munich, and the nearby Dachau concentration camp. The not so hidden agenda of the trip was to acquaint Jacqueline with the darker side of Europe so she wouldn't think that the old continent was all lively Left Bank cafés and Cote d'Azur beaches. To his credit, this had been Hughdie's idea. He had served in Naval Intelligence during World War II and knew well the horrors of Hitler's regime.

Then, contrary to her father's wishes, she ended her year in Europe with a three-week junket to Ireland and Scotland with Yusha Auchincloss.

Jack Bouvier had meanwhile undergone a serious cataract operation that had left him depleted, dispirited, and out of the action on the floor of the New York Stock Exchange for two months. He rented a cottage in East Hampton for July and August, counting on his daughters to visit him during his convalescence.

We can imagine how relieved and thankful he was when he received a telegram from Jacqueline on the *S.S. Liberté* announcing that she would be "home," in his apartment, shortly. Her ship would dock at 4 P.M. the following day at Pier 88, West 48th Street. His spirits soaring, Jack sent her a welcoming telegram:

CAN'T WAIT HURRY HURRY YOU CAN LEAVE EVERYTHING AT MY APARTMENT INCLUDING YOURSELF LOVE DAD

We can further imagine Jack's surprise and disappointment when he went down to the pier to await the *Liberté*'s docking and saw Jacqueline disembark with Yusha Auchincloss at her side. As it turned out, Jacqueline spent only two days with her father at his apartment and then, to Jack's further disappointment, took off for Merrywood and Washington. She enrolled for her senior year at George Washington University as a French literature major. She would be living with the Auchinclosses at Merrywood and commuting to Washington for her classes. Jacqueline's junior year abroad had made her fluent in French, widened her horizons, given her a greater sense of personal freedom, and had finally emancipated her from her father's control.

Chapter Eight

One Special Summer

*J*acqueline's decision to attend George Washington University
bitterly disappointed Jack Bouvier. It meant that Jacqueline was
now under Janet's control, and he probably would see very little of
his favorite daughter during the school year 1950–1951. I recall my
father telling us how despondent Jack was when Jacqueline
renounced Vassar: it caused him to assuage his pain by drinking
too many dry martinis with his customary veal chop at the New
York Stock Exchange Luncheon Club, to the inevitable detriment
of his business.

Jack was not incorrect in ascribing Jacqueline's decision to
leave Vassar to Janet's machinations. Janet had learned from
Jacqueline during her European trip with Hughdie to see her that
Jack was trying to persuade Jacqueline to live with him at 125 East
74th Street after she graduated. This had been enough to galvanize
Janet.

Janet was well aware of Jacqueline's growing love for Merrywood with its riding trails along the bluffs overlooking the Potomac and her dislike of Vassar's campus life. A year in Paris, living in
the midst of one of the world's greatest cities, rendered Poughkeepsie less bearable than before, and her delightful experience of
staying with a French family made dormitory life where she would

be just "a schoolgirl among schoolgirls" far less appealing than living in Merrywood and commuting to Washington. Accordingly, Jacqueline gave in to Mother's and Hughdie's wishes without immediately telling her father.

On her return to Washington, Janet marched over to the Dean of Admissions of George Washington University and persuaded him to accept all her daughter's previous college credits and allow her to graduate in two semesters as a French literature major. Jack Bouvier did not know it then, but he had been presented with a fait accompli.

Janet also hit on yet another way to keep Jacqueline away from Jack. Thumbing through an issue of *Vogue* magazine, she came across an announcement of *Vogue*'s sixteenth annual Prix de Paris writing contest, open to college seniors. The winner would be offered a one-year trainee position with the magazine: six months in Paris and six months in the magazine's New York offices. Janet brought the announcement to Jacqueline's attention and Jacqueline immediately requested the application forms.

The 1951 Prix de Paris competition required contestants to write a personal profile, four technical papers on fashion, a plan for a whole issue of *Vogue,* and a five-hundred-word essay on "People I Wish I Had Known." There were 1,280 applicants from 225 colleges. Jacqueline won first prize—a remarkable achievement for the twenty-two-year-old senior from George Washington University.

In light of what we now know about Jacqueline's early life, her personal profile is often more revealing for what it omits than what it includes. On the other hand it also reveals a refreshing honesty when it comes to evaluating her physical appearance and depicting her mother's incessant criticism and bossiness:

> I have no idea how to go about describing myself but perhaps with much sifting of wheat from chaff I can produce something fairly accurate.
>
> As to physical appearance, I am tall, 5′7″, with brown hair, a square face and eyes so unfortunately far apart that it takes three weeks to have a pair of glasses made with a

bridge wide enough to fit over my nose. I do not have a sensational figure but can look slim if I pick the right clothes. I flatter myself on being able at times to walk out of the house looking like the poor man's Paris copy, but often my mother will run up to inform me that my left stocking seam is crooked or the right-hand topcoat button about to fall off. This, I realize, is the Unforgivable Sin.

I lived in New York City until I was thirteen and spent the summers in the country. I hated dolls, loved horses and dogs and had skinned knees and braces on my teeth for what must have seemed an interminable length of time to my family.

I read a lot when I was little, much of which was too old for me. There were Chekhov and Shaw in the room where I had to take naps and I never slept but sat on the window sill reading, then scrubbed the soles of my feet so the nurse would not see I had been out of bed. My heroes were Byron, Mowgli, Robin Hood, Little Lord Fauntleroy's grandfather, and Scarlett O'Hara.

Growing up was not too painful a process. It happened gradually over the three years I spent at boarding school trying to imitate the girls who had callers every Saturday. I passed the finish line when I learned to smoke, in the balcony of the Normandie theatre in New York from a girl who pressed a Longfellow upon me then led me from the theatre when the usher told her that other people could not hear the film with so much coughing going on.

I spent two years at Vassar and cannot quite decide whether I liked it or not. I wish I had worked harder and gone away less on weekends. Last winter I took my Junior Year in Paris and spent the vacations in Austria and Spain. I loved it more than any year of my life. Being away from home gave me a chance to look at myself with a jaundiced eye. I learned not to be ashamed of a real hunger for knowledge, something I had always tried to hide, and I came home glad to start in here again but with a love for Europe that I am afraid will never leave me.

I suppose one should mention one's hobbies in a profile. I really don't have any that I work at constantly. I have studied art, here and in Paris, and I love to go to Art Exhibits and paint things that my mother doesn't put in the closet until a month after I have given them to her at Christmas. I have written a children's book for my younger brother and sister, as it amuses me to make up fairy tales and illustrate them. I love to ride and fox hunt in the open countryside.

Jacqueline was totally honest in describing her physical appearance in her late teens and early twenties. She was not typically "pretty," yet she was striking, as shown by her official *Vogue* portrait as the Prix de Paris winner. Her sister Lee was far prettier and had a more svelte figure. But Jacqueline had that strong broad face, that Greco-Roman chin, and those "eyes so unfortunately far apart" that would one day make her perhaps the most photogenic woman in the world.

Her mini-biography of her early years is so understated that you feel she must be hiding *something:* "I lived in New York City until I was thirteen and spent the summers in the country." No mention of the acrimonious and sometimes violent battles between her parents, of her mother's slapping her if she even mentioned she wanted to see her father, all of which, according to maids and governesses, often reduced her to tears. No mention of the wrenching separation and eventual divorce. And where "in the country" did she spend her summers? No words describing East Hampton or Newport. Was this understatement a coverup—an attempt to make it appear that she did not have such a privileged upbringing?

She was certainly forthright about her mother's incessant criticism. I had seen what Jacqueline went through with her mother's criticism of her appearance. Often at Sunday lunches, when Jacqueline would show up late on Lasata's terrace, Janet would greet her with: "Jackie, you look a sight, an absolute sight. Put

Jacqueline as pictured in Vogue *magazine, August 15, 1951, as the winner of* Vogue's *16th annual Prix de Paris writing contest for college seniors. (Photograph by Richard Rutledge. Courtesy* Vogue. *Copyright © 1951 [renewed 1979] by the Conde Nast Publications Inc.)*

some Band-Aids on your scraped knees for God's sake, and your hair looks like a bird's nest. Where have you *been?*"

Jackie had probably been at the stables; she would often race off to see her beloved horses as soon as she got out of church. Inevitably cobwebs, burrs, and horsehair would find their way into her thick, black mane.

Janet's criticism could be withering; as she grew older, Jackie sought to avoid it at all cost. Once, in the early years of her marriage to Jack Kennedy, she invited her mother to a small dinner party at the Kennedys' Georgetown townhouse and later observed: "I think I could entertain a king or queen with less apprehension than my mother, when there are other guests present."

It was especially revealing for Jacqueline to admit that she loved her junior year in Paris "more than any year of my life," that "being away from home gave me a chance to look at myself with a jaundiced eye." She might have added that being away also removed her from the incessant, and consequently distracting, tug-of-war between her mother and father. And being away from the American collegiate dating game unquestionably liberated Jacqueline from her compulsion to play dumb and keep her intellect under wraps so it wouldn't threaten a potential suitor. There is no doubt that the full awakening of Jacqueline's intellect and sensibilities occurred during her junior year abroad; she was liberated from the parochial, inbred, all-but-monastic life of the typical American college campus of her day.

Vogue also required its contestants to write four technical papers on fashion. Here is what Jacqueline wrote on an art she would one day epitomize to the entire world.

> *Fashions in Vogue are shown in three ways: (A) They are photographed on professional mannequins whose names are not given. (B) They are photographed on personalities, people in the news, and ladies of distinction and chic. . . . (C) They are drawn. . . . Which method do you prefer and why?*
>
> I prefer to see fashions photographed on professional models. A model's job is to efface herself and call attention to her dress. A woman of chic wishes to play up her own personality. She is well dressed if people say, "She looked heavenly but I can't remember what she had on." The readers of Vogue expect to learn something about a dress

before they trot off to Bonwit Teller or Julius Garfinckel and part with $89.95. . . .

If I am thinking of buying a dress I prefer to see it photographed on a professional model, but I think that Vogue would lose an enormous amount of its appeal were it to abandon sketches and clothes photographed on personalities. Variety is the spice of any good magazine and Vogue would be a bore if it offered nothing but poker-faced mannequins posturing through its pages. It would have the commercial deadliness of some wholesale buyer's magazine. It is fun to come across Marlene Dietrich brooding in a great black cape or Mrs. R. Fulton Cutting II sitting in a pink cloud of William Winkler nylon tulle. . . . Vogue's popularity is due to the variety of ways in which it presents fashions, but I should think that a survey would show that the clothes that sell the best are those that are photographed on professional models, and, offensive as the clink of a silver may be, Vogue could not exist if the clothes it featured did not sell.

If you could have any three of the fashions in this issue [August 15, 1950] to take back to college with you, which three would you choose and why?

The gray suit would be my uniform, would be fashionable and practical for as long as it held together. It could go traveling, shopping, to lunch and art exhibits with the accessories Vogue gave it. A head hugging veiled black velvet beehive hat, perhaps a hint of velvet at the throat and a dressy pin, black shoes, bag, and gloves and a big fur muff could take it cocktailing and even out for a non-dressy evening in the city. It could be dressed up or down. . . . The sleeveless plaid dress would fill the casual requirement in my wardrobe and would also be heaven-sent on occasions that hover between the casual and the "just a little dressy" when you never are quite sure of what to wear. It could go to football games or into the country under big coats. Worn over the black turtleneck blouse that I would buy for the gray suit, and with a black belt it could cope with Sunday afternoons at a college followed by dinner in town, or with Sunday lunch at his family's house in the country. . . . The black top and orange taffeta skirt would see me through after football game dances in fraternity houses when the boys don't dress, and through dinner, theatre and dancing dates in the city. Because they are separates I could get at least two more dresses out of them. . . .

Make out a plan of beauty care suitable for a college girl.
You can never slip into too dismal an abyss of untidiness if once every seven days you will pull yourself up short and cope with ragged ends. Thursday night, the night before a weekend, is a good one for this sort of overhauling. If you will allot two hours to a thorough going over and regard these two hours as sacrosanct as any of your classes, you can avoid smudged nails daubed on the New York Central from a bottle of polish that has spilled in your pocketbook, strange unwanted waves in your hair because you have washed it at midnight and gone to bed too tired to wait for it to dry, stubbly legs with razor cuts, and a legion of other horrors. . . . If you will buy decent materials and take care of them (no dirty powder puff, unwashed brush and comb, dried out nail polish), eat and sleep sensibly, remember that cleanliness and neatness are what you are working for, and that they can be attained with ten minutes of washing and brushing a day and a little extra time one night a week, you should never have to scream in anguish and take an hour to get ready when told that your best beau has arrived unexpectedly and is waiting downstairs.

What is your opinion of the perfume presentation in the December Vogue? Suggest, in 300 words or more, an alternative presentation.
Perfume was just as effective in piquing the male olfactory glands before our era of adjective laden advertisements.

Why not quote some of the poetry it has inspired? It also is analogous to wine. Both are liquids that act upon the closely related sense of taste and smell to produce an intoxicating effect. Wine has had an even stronger appeal in literature, from Omar Khayam to Colonel Cantwell and Renata. Why not pilfer some of its drawing power and incorporate it into an article on perfume? . . . An analogy of wine and perfume, entitled "Intoxicating Liquids," "The Petal and the Grape," etc. would be done in much the same way. The left hand page would show the compartments of a wine cellar. In each compartment a bottle of perfume would be standing upright. The label beneath it would say "Lentheric—Numero 6, 1950" in the same way that wines are catalogued. This layout would be most effective in black and white photography with the black depths of the compartments pointing up the reflections of the glass bottles. The right hand page—also with black background—would show some strewn flower petals, a thin-stemmed crystal wineglass with the blurred suggestion of a woman (a long neck, an earring, her hand) pouring perfume out of a Diorama bottle into the glass. Again in the right hand corner would be a few lines of copy stressing the analogy between perfume and wine.

Suggest a new approach for Vogue on the subject of men's fashions. Any new approach to men's fashions should be directed at women. Most women know relatively little about men's clothing. Why not teach them something about the male wardrobe in a series of articles, so that at Christmas and birthdays they will no longer present the man in their life with a neatly wrapped sartorial blunder. . . . The little details that make a man a fashion plate could be brought out by a series of "good and bad" photographs. Well dressed personalities in the news, such as Dean Acheson, Anthony Eden, Fred Astaire, could be shown beside badly dressed models. Thus the importance of a well cut lapel, a neatly folded handkerchief, tapering as opposed to peg-cut trousers, the amount of cuff visible below the sleeve could be made clear to women. . . .

It seems to me that any woman would welcome a few pointers on men's clothes. She is eager to brighten up her husband's wardrobe but does not know how to go about it without descending to the robin's-egg blue gabardine suit and hand-painted tie level. If Vogue shows her how she can introduce color and variety into his wardrobe and still remain within the bounds of convention and good taste she will be grateful, and will welcome the death knell of the adage "Clothes make the man, but not when a woman chooses the clothes."

Jacqueline's advice on fashion was obviously designed to ingratiate herself with *Vogue* editors. Her People-I-Wish-I-Had-Known essay showed a less practical, more whimsical side to her character. She was specifically asked to "include your favorite people in the world of art, literature, or other milieus, no longer living, and to give reasons for your selections." She wrote:

Putting them in chronological order, I would say that the three men I should most like to have known were Charles Baudelaire, Oscar Wilde, and Diaghileff. They followed close upon each other in the three quarters of a century from 1850–1925. They came from three different countries and specialized in three different fields: poetry, playwrighting, and ballet, yet I think a common theory runs through their work, a certain concept of the interrelation of the arts. . . .

Baudelaire and Wilde were both rich men's sons who lived like dandies, ran through what they had, and died in extreme poverty. Both were poets and idealists who could paint sinfulness with honesty and still believe in something higher. The Frenchman, an isolated genius who could have lived at any time, used as his weapons venom and despair. Wilde, who typified the late Victorian era, could, with the flash of an epigram, bring about what serious reformers had for years been trying to accomplish. . . . Serge Diaghileff dealt not with the interaction of the senses but with an interaction of the arts, an interaction of the cultures of East and West. Though not an artist himself, he possessed what is rarer than artistic genius in any one field, the sensitivity to take the best of each man and incorporate it into a masterpiece all the more precious because it lives only in the minds of those who have seen it and disintegrates as soon as he is gone. . . .

It is because I love the works of these three men that I wish I had known them. If I could be a sort of Overall Art Director of the Twentieth Century, watching everything from a chair hanging in space, it is their theories of art that I would apply to my period, their poems that I would have music and paintings and ballets composed to. And they would make such good stepping-stones if we thought we could climb any higher.

So here the twenty-two-year-old, highly talented Jacqueline Bouvier wins the coveted *Vogue* Prix de Paris over 1,280 other contestants and what does she do? She turns it down. As she later explained it:

> I guess I was too scared to go to Paris again. I felt then that if I went back, I'd live there forever. I loved Paris so much. That's such a formative year when you get out of college.

I believe the translation of this excuse is that Hughdie and Janet were only too well aware that winning the Prix de Paris meant that Jackie would be obliged to spend six months in Paris and six months at *Vogue*'s offices *in New York*. That, of course, meant that Jacqueline would once more fall under the potent influence of Black Jack, that she might even spend those six months staying at Jack's apartment. This wouldn't do. Stating publicly that they feared Jacqueline might become an expatriate if she accepted *Vogue's* offer—*Vogue* did, after all, have an office in Paris in which Jacqueline could easily find work—they decided it would be best if Jackie remained in Washington.

To assuage Jacqueline's disappointment, Janet and Hughdie decided they would finance a trip to Europe for Jacqueline and Lee during the following summer, after Jackie graduated from George Washington and Lee graduated from Miss Porter's. The trip was to be a dual graduation present.

A few days before their departure, Jacqueline was introduced to John F. Kennedy by a mutual friend, Charles Bartlett, a Washington correspondent for the *Chattanooga Times* who had attended Yale. The meeting occurred during a small dinner party given by the Bartletts in Georgetown, and the boyish congressman from Massachusetts and the recent George Washington University graduate barely said a word to each other.

Jacqueline and Lee Bouvier departed from New York on June 7, 1951, aboard the *Queen Elizabeth.* I remember envying them their trip, for I was compelled to spend that summer completing my naval training at the Reserve Officers Candidate School on Treasure Island in San Francisco Bay, a bleak prospect in comparison to the delights awaiting Jacqueline and Lee.

Jacqueline was twenty-two and Lee seventeen. Early on, the two girls decided to write and illustrate an account of their travels that they would present to Janet and Hughdie when they returned as an expression of their gratitude. Jackie would do the drawings, write the poetry, and narrate their travels in Rome and Spain. It would fall to Lee to describe their adventures on the *Queen Elizabeth* and in London, Paris, Venice, Rome, and Florence.

In *One Special Summer* Jacqueline comes across as droll, arch, irreverent, whimsical and sarcastic, while Lee reveals herself to be surprisingly serious. In her introduction to the book, Lee wrote that her study of art history at Miss Porter's School had inspired her with a fascination for the Italian Renaissance; so much so that

> out of the blue, at the age of fifteen I had started a correspondence with the great art historian Bernard Berenson.

To my delight and amazement he replied, and ever since
the first exchange of letters, one of my greatest wishes was
to go to Florence and meet him.

I read Berenson's *Italian Painters of the Renaissance* at Princeton
and admired him very much, but will admit that I never had the
nerve to write him. Lee, at fifteen, was either precocious or star-
struck—probably both.

Janet and Uncle Hughdie financed the Bouvier sisters' summer in
Europe, but they did not spoil them by arranging excessively luxu-
rious accommodations. The girls traveled third class on the *Queen
Elizabeth* and were forever getting into trouble trying to crash into
first class. In Europe, they did not always stay in first- or second-
class hotels, but Uncle Hughdie did provide letters of credit at
American Express in London, Paris, Madrid, Nice, Rome, and
Lucerne and at the Chase Bank in Paris.

The Bouvier sisters did some serious sightseeing in London
and Paris, but their book reflects not so much what they saw and
learned in museums and palaces as what "hilarious" social adventures they had at parties and the cafés.

Uncle Hughdie was particularly anxious that his stepdaughters represent their country in a dignified way. They assured him in
a preface to their book that they would.

I know you are right about us representing our country
and that we must never do anything that would call attention to us and make people shocked at Americans. We DO
sew on all our buttons and wear gloves and never go out in
big cities except in what we would wear to church in
Newport on Sundays.

The book's most serious part was Lee's interview and
descriptions of her hero, Bernard Berenson. She and Jacqueline
visited the venerable renaissance art historian and collector at his

sixteenth-century Florence villa, I Tatti, which now belongs to Harvard University.

Berenson's first question to the Bouvier sisters, as reported by Lee, was, "Why did Mummy divorce Daddy?" No answer was given, or at least not one related in *One Special Summer*. Berenson went on to give the Bouvier sisters some marital advice. "Never follow your senses," he told them, "marry someone who will constantly stimulate you—and you him."

Among Berenson's remarks that most impressed the Bouvier sisters were: "The only way to exist happily is to love your work"; "Anything you want you must make enemies and suffer for"; and "Don't waste your time with Life Diminishing people, seek the company of Life Enhancing people. . . . If you find it's often you are with unstimulating people it must because you yourself are not stimulating."

The Bouvier sisters' next adventure was in Spain. They had an audience in Madrid with the Spanish Ambassador, who promptly invited them to a reception for "THE SENATORS!!" Jackie described this encounter with the august U.S. senators abroad in amused tones, particularly when recalling the behavior of one persistent, buffoonish senator who latched on to Lee early in the proceedings and couldn't be shaken off. Obviously totally unaware of the sisters' background, he ended by offering to take them to lunch at the Senate cafeteria if they ever came to Washington—to bring a little pleasure into their lives.

More minor adventures in Spain followed. Then it was time to return home. They docked in New York on September 15, 1951, in time for Lee to enter Sarah Lawrence as a freshman and Jacqueline to embark on her first paying job.

As it would turn out, Jackie's and Lee's tour of Europe in the summer of 1951 was but a prelude to a series of much grander travels together. As Lee wrote in her postscript when the book was eventually published, she accompanied Jackie—then the First Lady—on her trip to Rome, India, and Pakistan. She also recalled:

In 1963 Jackie and I took another trip, this time to
Morocco. We were the guests of the King. . . . At one
point Jackie forced me to sing "In an Old Dutch Garden
Where the Tulips Grow" to the King's harem. . . . It was
one moment of Jackie's humor I didn't share when I heard
her announcing that her sister had a lovely voice and
would now proceed to sing.

Jacqueline and Lee presented their whimsical account to Janet
and Uncle Hughdie upon their return home. The illustrated manuscript languished in the attic of Hammersmith Farm from 1951
to 1973, until Lee got the idea of publishing it in book form and
persuaded Eleanor Friede of Delacorte Press to buy it. Lee col-
lected a $100,000 advance from Delacorte as well as a contract
with the Book-of-the-Month Club for 100,000 copies. The book
came out in October 1974, but it soon became apparent that it was
not going to enjoy much of a sale. It did not come even close to
earning its advance.

What author and publisher did not realize at the time was
that by 1974 much of the glow had faded from the Bouvier-
Kennedy image. The public never approved of Jacqueline's marriage to Onassis, were appalled by the Kennedy-Onassis-Callas
shenanigans, and looked down on Lee's post Radziwill divorce
antics with the likes of Truman Capote and Andy Warhol. In the
end, people did not buy the book because, even though it was
highly entertaining, they had become somewhat disenchanted with
its authors. Jacqueline's image did not regain its former luster until
several years after Onassis died in 1975, the beginning of her career
as an editor at Viking and later at Doubleday, and the reputation
she gained in the 1980s as an exceptional mother. As for Lee,
when *One Special Summer* came out in 1974, she had done little or
nothing to ingratiate herself with the American reading public.

Chapter Nine

The Inquiring
Camera Girl

When Jackie and Lee returned to New York after their special summer, Lee knew precisely what she was going to do, while Jackie was still in a quandary about her immediate future. Lee enrolled as a freshman at Sarah Lawrence College in Bronxville, eager to pursue her studies in art history, for which she had received such a bolt of inspiration from Bernard Berenson. Jacqueline floated back to Hammersmith Farm and the Newport social world that bored her so.

At about the same time—late September 1951—I reported to my ship in Norfolk, Virginia, after having just earned my commission as a naval officer in San Francisco. Soon my ship was on its way to join the U.S. Sixth Fleet in the Mediterranean, and there followed a period during which I lost all contact with Jacqueline save what my parents reported back to me about her from time to time, for they remained in continuous touch with her father.

I recall my father writing how bitterly disappointed Uncle Jack was when Jacqueline once again refused his offer to have her come live with him and work downtown in his brokerage business (whose offices were contiguous with my father's). One letter contained a note from my mother telling me she had been down to Jack's somewhat unkempt apartment and was astonished at how many pictures he had of Jackie on his walls and furniture. I would receive letters from my parents in Gibraltar, Genoa, Naples, and Palermo about Uncle Jack's increasing desolation over his separation from his daughters, and his gradual descent into a reclusive (and ever more alcoholic) existence.

I did not catch up with Jacqueline again until November 1952, when, by a flukish set of circumstances, the Navy sent me to the Pentagon, on "temporary additional duty," precisely at the time Jacqueline had begun dating John F. Kennedy seriously and there was talk all over Washington that they were going to get engaged.

In October 1951, Jacqueline returned to Merrywood with the entire Auchincloss clan, with no particular plans in mind, and resumed one of her favorite sports, fox hunting in the Virginia countryside. On one of these hunts, she was thrown from her mount and knocked unconscious.

When Jack Bouvier heard about the accident, he wrote his daughter a sympathetic but stern letter, telling her that her narrow escape should have taught her a lesson. He went over her history of hunting mishaps, recalling that she had broken her collarbone when she was thirteen and had suffered a slipped disc while riding Danseuse at Vassar. He admonished her to give up fox hunting—or else he would stop sending her monthly allowance.

By mid-December, Jacqueline had recovered sufficiently to start thinking seriously about what she was going to do with her life. She regretted not having accepted the *Vogue* Prix de Paris, since it had offered such an exceptional opportunity and she had always been interested in journalism. Fortunately, Uncle Hughdie came to the rescue.

Through his friend, Arthur Krock of the *New York Times,* who was also a good friend of Joseph P. Kennedy, Hughdie arranged for Jacqueline to be interviewed by Frank Waldrop, Editor-in-Chief and one of the owners of the now defunct *Washington Times-Herald.* Waldrop, who had once employed Joseph P. Kennedy's ill-fated daughter Kathleen "Kick" Kennedy, was evidently quite impressed with Jacqueline and offered her a trainee job in late December 1951. She would run errands and do odd jobs for various reporters and editors. She soon graduated to the position of Inquiring

Photografer, without a by-line, at $42.50 a week. So capable was she at operating her bulky Speed Flash Graflex camera and concocting unusually provocative questions that by March 26, 1952, her name headed her column.

Also at this time, Jacqueline's romance with the young stockbroker, John G. W. Husted, was heating up. Husted had given her a diamond-and-sapphire engagement ring and had a talk with Jack Bouvier at his apartment. Jack was delighted with the idea of having a fellow stockbroker as a son-in-law, especially because it meant that Jackie would be living in New York, far from the Auchincloss camp. As I've mentioned, Janet found Husted not wealthy enough for her daughter and forbade Jacqueline to marry him.

The breakup of her relationship with Husted didn't seem to bother Jacqueline much. She was enjoying her full-time job as Inquiring Photografer, and, since she was living at Merrywood, she didn't have to pay room and board—her $42.50 a week was all gravy. Her only fixed expense was gas for the secondhand, black Mercury convertible she used for commuting to work, and she was meeting a lot of interesting people who took her to lunch. In April 1952, the young congressman she had been introduced to almost a year before announced that he would run for the Senate in November. On May 8, 1952, their mutual friends, Charles and Martha Bartlett, brought them together again at a dinner party. This time the two suddenly clicked and began seeing each other, if not regularly, at least sporadically.

Like Jacqueline, I too was discovering new vistas not previously experienced. As the assistant navigator of a warship with the U.S. Sixth Fleet in the Mediterranean, I was putting into ports I had dreamed of all my life: Malaga, Marseilles, Nice, Cannes, Genoa, and Naples on the mainland; Catania, Augusta, Siracusa, Trapani, and Palermo in Sicily, and, in the Eastern Mediterranean, Piraeus, the port of Athens, and Istanbul. The Mediterranean in those postwar years had become "Mare Nostrum," an American lake, and we were accorded royal treatment everywhere.

Since I was the only officer aboard ship who had a liberal arts education—at Princeton I had been a history major—and had evinced a knowledge of the history of the ports we were visiting, the captain gave me the collateral duty of ship's guide ashore. Whenever we put into a port, I would shepherd groups of sailors to the great historical and artistic monuments of the city and its environs.

My most adventurous feat was leading about fifty sailors on a climb through ashes and lava to the smoking crater of Mt. Etna, Europe's most active volcano, which towered 11,000 feet above the East Coast of Sicily. Not long after, our Navigator became incapacitated and the captain appointed me to take his place. I had the thrill of navigating our ship from the Aegean, up the narrow, winding Dardanelles along with brightly painted dhows with lateen sails, and through the Sea of Marmara to suddenly behold the minarets and domes of the great mosques of Istanbul rising beside the Golden Horn.

When our ship finally returned to Newport News, Virginia, for dry-dock repairs, the captain decided to put his ship's historian and tour guide to good use. He dispatched me to the Navy Department at the Pentagon to research and write a history of our ship.

It was in early November 1952 that I went to Washington on this assignment. By then I had been made aware by my parents that Jacqueline was seeing a good deal of Congressman John F. Kennedy during the summer and fall. There was even talk of their getting engaged. Because I had always loved and admired Jackie, and had long regarded her as almost a sister, I remember being very anxious to see her again. I phoned her at Merrywood and we made a date to have lunch.

By then Jacqueline had been promoted from Inquiring Photografer to the position of Inquiring Camera Girl at the *Times-Herald* and had received a raise from $42.50 to $56.75 a week. These were momentous times for the Kennedy family as well as the nation. John F. Kennedy, the thirty-four-year-old congressman from the eleventh district of Massachusetts, had narrowly defeated the seemingly entrenched Republican incumbent senator, Henry Cabot Lodge, in the November 4, 1952, elections, and General Dwight D. Eisenhower, heading the Republican ticket, had beaten

Jacqueline Bouvier, Inquiring Camera Girl for the Washington Times-Herald, *photographing the newly elected senator from Massachusetts, John F. Kennedy, in Washington, November 1952.*

Adlai Stevenson for the presidency. Inquiring Camera Girl Jacqueline Bouvier was busy asking the departing treasurer of the United States, the secretary of the Senate, an administrative assistant to the president, Perle Mesta, and the attorney general what they would be doing after Eisenhower's inauguration.

Jacqueline and I finally met for lunch during the first week of November 1952 at the restaurant in the Mayflower Hotel. I had not seen her since that 1949 summer when I was a cadet in Newport training to be a naval officer. Three years had passed and

I noticed how dramatically she had changed. No longer the some-what superficial society girl and shy, restrained prisoner of the Auchinclosses, she seemed much more relaxed, much more cheer-ful, and far more beautiful. She now enjoyed an added degree of freedom, had some money in her purse, and was meeting many interesting people in her capacity as Inquiring Camera Girl.

I noticed she had lost some weight, particularly from her face. Her puffy teenager cheeks were gone—the contours of her face now had some definition. Her high cheekbones were more in evidence, as were her jutting Greco-Roman chin, wide-apart eyes, and incredibly thick, dark hair. She truly was a woman now, impos-ing, witty, charming, and with a somewhat arch sense of humor. To be made fun of by Jacqueline was always a veiled compliment—she had a tendency to ridicule people she really liked.

After chatting about various members of the family and lamenting the loss of Lasata, I asked if there was any truth to the rumors I had heard that she and Jack Kennedy were getting very serious about each other.

"Mother has mentioned it to me several times since I returned to the States," I said, "and there's certainly a lot of scuttle-butt over at the Pentagon about it. Remember Kennedy's an old navy man."

When she laughed, I knew right away that if she was taking him seriously, she was not going to tell me.

"You know, he's become so vain he has to have a hairdresser come in practically every day," she giggled, "so his hair will always look bushy and fluffy."

"Well, I suppose that goes with being a politician today," I returned. "They're always before the TV cameras. They have to appear like movie stars."

"Just think what it's going to be like now that he's become a *senator*," she said in that low, breathless voice. "You know already if when we go out together to a party, or reception, or something, nobody recognizes him, or no photographer takes his picture, he sulks afterwards for *hours*."

"I guess he's very ambitious. Today a rising politician has to fight for attention."

"Oh sure, he's ambitious, all right," she said. "He even told me he intends to be president some day," and she laughed again.

Her mirth told me she liked Kennedy a lot and was having a good time with him. Jacqueline had a way of not taking men seriously, even when she liked them.

After a while, our conversation drifted back to our Bouvier relatives. I recall that Jackie was particularly interested in knowing how our bohemian Aunt Edie and her beautiful thirty-five-year-old daughter Little Edie were getting along in their rundown East Hampton mansion, Grey Gardens, with its forty cats. Evidently, she had not heard anything about the two Ediths for some time.

She laughingly talked about introducing Jack Kennedy to Big and Little Edie some day, remarking that "the cat hairs in the house alone would drive him crazy" because he was allergic to animal hair, especially horse hair. "Imagine me with someone allergic to horses!" she exclaimed, and we enjoyed a good laugh over that.

I was attempting to grill her more on her rumored romance when she suddenly cut me off by taking my picture with her huge Speed Graflex and asking me a question for her newspaper column. The question: "Are men as inclined to fall for a 'line' as girls are?" My fifty-word answer and photograph, which appeared in the November 11, 1952, Inquiring Photografer column of the *Times-Herald,* amounted to a qualified "Yes."

In January 1953, John F. Kennedy took his seat in the U.S. Senate and General Eisenhower was inaugurated as the nation's thirty-fourth president. On the evening of January 20, Senator Kennedy escorted Jacqueline Bouvier to Eisenhower's Inaugural Ball, an act that many felt was a portent of their eventual engagement and marriage.

I believe it was Jack Kennedy's tremendous victory over the seemingly unbeatable Henry Cabot Lodge in the senatorial election

Inquiring Photografer

By JACQUELINE BOUVIER

THE QUESTION

Are men as inclined to fall for a "line" as girls are? Asked on Connecticut Ave. NW.

THE ANSWERS

Ensign John Davis, Norfolk: More so, because they don't get them as often. When our ship was in the Mediterranean, we wanted to appear continental and not like American tourists. If any girl said "Oh, you look so Turkish," or "I'd have taken you for a Neapolitan," why I fell for it like a ton of bricks.

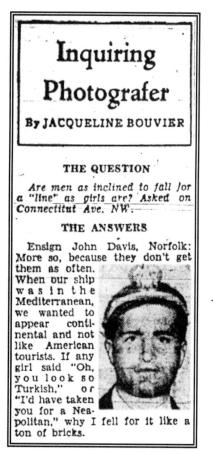

From early 1952 to June 1953 Jacqueline Bouvier worked first as the Inquiring Photografer and then as the Inquiring Camera Girl for the now defunct Washington Times-Herald. *It was her first job, with a starting salary of $42.50 a week. She interviewed the author, who was a naval officer at the time, when they met for lunch in Washington on November 11, 1952.*

that convinced Jacqueline that the somewhat ineffectual congressman from Massachusetts had what it took to perhaps go all the way to the White House someday.

An unmistakable sign that Jackie was now taking Jack Kennedy seriously came in February 1953 when Kennedy went to New York to meet Jackie's father.

Jack Bouvier was suffering acutely from the loss of his hold on his daughters. Lee was about to get engaged to Michael Canfield, the adopted son of publisher Cass Canfield, president of Harper & Row. Jackie was on the verge of becoming engaged to Kennedy.

Inquiring Camera Girl

By JACQUELINE BOUVIER

THE QUESTION

What's it like observing the pages at close range? Asked of senators and the Vice President.

THE ANSWERS

Vice President Richard M. Nixon: I would predict that some future states-man will come from the ranks of the page corps. During my time as a senator, I noticed that they are very quick boys, most of whom have a definite interest in politics. I feel they could not get a better political grounding than by witnessing the Senate in session day after day as they do.

Sen. John F. Kennedy (D) of Massachusetts: I've often thought that the country might be better off if we Senators and the pages traded jobs. If such legislation is ever enacted I'll be glad to hand over the reins to Jerry Hoobler.' In the meantime, I think he might be just the fellow to help me straighten out my relationship with the cops. I've often mistaken Jerry for a senator because he looks so old.

THE QUESTION

What's it like observing senators at close range? Asked of Senate pages.

THE ANSWERS

Gary Hegelson, Wisconsin: We've got this book with pictures of senators in it and I'm trying to get their autographs. I didn't know when I could get Nixon, he's so busy. One day when he was presiding over the Senate and I was sitting on the rostrum I decided that was my chance. He signed it right away.

Jerry Hoobler of Ohio: Senator Kennedy always brings his lunch in a brown paper bag. I guess he eats it in his office. I see him with it every morning when I'm on the elevator. He's always being mistaken for a tourist by the cops because he looks so young. The other day he wanted to use the special phones, and they told him, "Sorry, mister, but these are reserved for senators."

Promoted to Inquiring Camera Girl, with her salary increased to $56.75 a week, Jacqueline interviewed Vice President Nixon and Senator Kennedy after Congress reconvened in early 1953.

Once married, his girls would no longer be dependent on him for anything—not for their allowances, not for his department store charge accounts, not for his company, and not even for his love.

I am certain that Uncle Jack did not have an incestuous relationship with Jacqueline, but I am just as certain that he was deeply and passionately *in love* with her. She was the light of his life, the meaning of his existence. She and Lee were everything to him. As Lee so movingly said after his death in 1957:

> We were his life. He never created another life for himself, except us. His children grew up and went their ways. He became more and more of a recluse. My father always felt he was a failure in some way. In the end he was a heartbreaking figure.

Jack Bouvier, a diehard Republican, was prepared to dislike Jack Kennedy because he so detested his father. Joe Kennedy had not only been a New Deal Democrat who, when he was ambassador to Great Britain, advised Roosevelt to appease Hitler and dissuade Churchill from going to war against him, but, as chairman of the Securities and Exchange Commission, he had initiated certain practices that had been detrimental to Black Jack's business, costing him considerable loss of income.

To his surprise, and Jackie's delight, the two Jacks hit it off beautifully. Their first meeting was over dinner in February 1953 in a midtown restaurant. Later Jackie stated, "They were very much alike. They talked about sports, politics, and women—what all red-blooded men like to talk about."

Louis Ehret, a good friend of Jack Bouvier, told author David Heymann that Black Jack told him that "aside from needing a haircut, young Mr. Kennedy seemed a decent chap—not what I expected. I thought he'd be more like his old man. At any rate, Jackie's madly in love with him."

On other visits to New York, Kennedy made a point of solidifying his relationship with Jackie's father. He accepted an invitation from Black Jack to have lunch with him at the Stock

Exchange Luncheon Club and take a tour of the Exchange's frantic trading floor. And Black Jack had his future son-in-law up to his apartment on 74th Street for dinner one evening, where they watched a prize fight on a television set entirely surrounded by photos of Jackie.

Although he still remained fearful of losing Jacqueline to the huge and powerful Kennedy clan, Black Jack was satisfied that he could get along well enough with the young senator so that his eventual marriage to his daughter would not alienate her from him entirely. It was, however, small consolation.

When I first met Jack Kennedy, in the Senate cafeteria, through Jacqueline's auspices, I soon realized how easy it was to get along with him. I was also quite surprised by how disarmingly young he looked for a man in his mid-thirties. He was, first of all, extraordinarily thin. Although he had a few lines at the corners of his eyes, the sort one gets from squinting into the sun too often, his great shock of reddish-brown hair, practically standing on end at the front of his head, made him look like someone far younger. Later, when I became aware he was a victim of Addison's disease, I was told by a doctor that an abnormally youthful appearance was characteristic of most Addisonians.

The most salient characteristic of Jack Kennedy's personality, I quickly learned, was his unobtrusiveness. He was not aggressive in conversation, but was instead a great listener who gave you his undivided attention and seemed genuinely interested in everything you said. He was, in essence, the antithesis of the typical overbearing politician. Kennedy was a quiet, reflective man. I recall he was very interested in the NATO maneuvers I had participated in while on duty with the Sixth Fleet in the Mediterranean. "That's one of my goals in the Senate," he observed, "to help make sure NATO really *works,* that the alliance develops genuine teamwork and cohesiveness in the face of the godawful threat we face from the Soviet bloc."

After a while, our conversation drifted to women. I remember he told me what "a terrific girl" Jackie was and then asked me what I thought of the Italian, Sicilian, Greek, and Turkish women

I met in the Mediterranean. Who were the hottest? I replied that unquestionably the Sicilian girls were, but they were also the most dangerous, because they wanted us to get them pregnant so that we would be forced to marry them and eventually take them back to the States. When I told him that the commanding officers of ships in the Sixth Fleet strongly discouraged us from seeing Sicilian women, he seemed to get a kick out of this, and recalled that when he was in the Navy in the Pacific, the only women available were "illiterate primitives" and nurses. When we parted, he complained that he now had to sit through a long hearing on labor that had bored him "shitless" all morning.

As the relationship between Jacqueline and Jack Kennedy unfolded slowly, step by step, Lee Bouvier was rushing as fast as she could into marriage with young Michael Canfield, who had been appointed to the staff of Winthrop Aldrich, the American ambassador to Great Britain, and had given up his editorial job at Harper & Row.

Lee had known Canfield since her debutante days, when, like Jackie, she had been proclaimed Debutante of the Year by Cholly Knickerbocker. Michael had been a senior at Harvard then, a tall (6′3″), elegant young man, rumored to be the illegitimate son of the Duke of Kent, whom he closely resembled. Before going to Harvard, he had served in the Marine Corps and participated in the bloody battle of Iwo Jima.

Lee became seriously involved with him when she was working as a special assistant to Diana Vreeland, head of the fashion department of *Harper's Bazaar,* after she dropped out of Sarah Lawrence in her sophomore year. Her relentless but amicable rivalry with Jackie was driving her to get married before her sister at any cost. Mother Janet was worried about Michael's financial prospects. Even though he was the son of the head of a venerable publishing house, it would be a while before he could earn much of a living from being an editor. As for Canfield, he was under the impression that Lee was rich, not knowing that Hughdie Auchincloss had not included her in his will or that Jack Bouvier's finances had been steadily declining. All Lee really had in terms of money was the $3,000 her grandfather had left her and her salary at *Harper's Bazaar.* Notwithstanding these mutual misconceptions, Lee and Michael became engaged and set April 18, 1953, as their wedding day.

I did not attend the wedding because I was off again on joint NATO maneuvers in the Mediterranean with the Sixth Fleet, my second tour of duty in the "Med," but my mother and her twin Michelle went and wrote me detailed accounts of the ceremony in Washington and the reception at Merrywood.

Their big worry—and everyone else's—was how Jack Bouvier would hold up in the company of the detested Auchinclosses. Would he be able to give his daughter away with dignity and composure?

It was decided that his twin sisters would be in charge of Jack from the time he left Pennsylvania Station to his arrival at Holy Trinity Church in Georgetown and finally to the ordeal at Merrywood. They dutifully did not allow him to go to the club car, even to eat. They brought along his favorite tomato and watercress sandwiches. From Union Station, they shepherded him to the church, where, under the anxious eyes of his sisters, Jacqueline, Janet, Uncle Hughdie, and all the other Auchinclosses, he guided Lee up the aisle with a sure step and all the Bouvier dignity, he could muster, which was considerable. He gave away his younger daughter—she was only twenty—to Michael Canfield in great style.

The lavish Merrywood reception was next, and again the twins kept Jack under strict control, never leaving his side for a second. With great patience, they had listened to him rail against Janet, Old Man Lee, and the Auchinclosses for three hours on the train to Washington, so by the time he arrived at Merrywood he was all talked out. Once in the heart of Auchincloss country he became almost demure. My mother allowed him only one drink, a shot of vodka in a tall glass of mineral water, and told the waiters not to serve him again.

After steeling himself to shake hands with Janet, Hughdie, and Old Man Lee, and giving Jackie and Lee big hugs, he greeted several of the guests he knew, took Lee out on the dance floor for a twirl, and then went for a tour of the Auchincloss estate with the twins. It was a cool, cloudy April afternoon, but, according to my mother, Merrywood never looked more beautiful. The great Georgian mansion was surrounded by rolling green meadows and clumps of budding trees, the countryside through which Jackie loved to ride, and, in the distance, the serene Potomac. Jack had to concede that the estate was every bit as beautiful as Lasata at the height of its glory.

Later, when he returned to the reception to say his good-byes, just as Lee was throwing her bouquet to Jackie, he almost broke down. He had finally seen what his rival had been able to give Jackie and Lee for the past ten years. On their way to Union Station, the twins noticed that he was uncustomarily silent.

After Lee's wedding, Jacqueline experienced the uncomfortable feeling of being the older, unmarried sister. In those days, when the only acceptable career for a woman was housewife and mother, she was now a young "old maid." Consequently, she felt compelled to bring her maddeningly spasmodic relationship with Jack Kennedy to a head and get him to propose.

She thought she had laid the groundwork for her acceptance by the Kennedy family during the previous summer when she had been invited to the Kennedy compound in Hyannis Port. She sensed she had to somehow impress the entire clan, from old Joe Kennedy and his wife Rose down to twenty-year-old Teddy. It was not easy for the reticent, introspective Jacqueline, who once confessed she always felt like an outsider in American life, to confront this huge, aggressively ambitious clan whose family ethos was a near-maniacal urge to "win, win, win, at any cost."

By 1952, the family had lost Joe Jr. to a near-suicidal bombing run in World War II, and in 1948 Kathleen "Kick" Kennedy to another near-suicidal air accident in the Crevennes Mountains in the Ardeche, France. In 1941, at the insistence of Father Joe, an unnecessary prefrontal lobotomy had been performed on the mildly retarded Rosemary Kennedy, rendering her virtually a vegetable.

Thus, by the time Jacqueline was introduced to the family, the Kennedys had already suffered a number of tragedies, and patriarch Joseph P. Kennedy was determined to make up for them. He was going to propel his second son, Jack, into the White House. Jack had already proven himself a tough political candidate, winning two elections to the House of Representatives by large margins. Now, in the summer of 1952, he was getting ready for his fall campaign against Henry Cabot Lodge for a Senate seat. If he could beat Lodge, Joe figured, he could beat anyone.

Joe Kennedy knew that if he got Jack elected to the Senate, it would only be a matter of time before he would run him for the presidency. To do that, Jack would need a suitable wife. Joe Kennedy was well aware of Jacqueline Bouvier's credentials, that she was a "society girl" who had been nominated Debutante of the Year by the top gossip columnist of the Hearst papers, that she had done well in her studies at Vassar, had been selected for the Smith Group Junior Year Abroad Program, had also done well at the Sorbonne, and subsequently won *Vogue*'s prestigious Prix de Paris. Now he was going to judge her as a person, to see whether she had what it took to be First Lady of the United States.

At the age of twenty-three, Jacqueline had become a shrewd judge of character; she had learned, from her experience of juggling the demands of Janet and Hughdie with those of her father, how to manipulate people. In her first meetings with Joe Kennedy, Jackie poured on the charm and played on the insecurities of the once-poor Irish boy born in the East Boston boondocks. No doubt she, or Jack, alluded to her supposed aristocratic French-Catholic background and did not divulge her mother's 100-percent Irish ancestry. She might have mentioned the myth Janet was fond of propagating, that her family came from the "Lees of Maryland, an aristocratic offshoot of the Lees of Virginia." To the social-climbing Joe Kennedy she wanted to represent upper-class status, and so she emphasized her sense of style in dress, jewelry, makeup, and manners. This ploy impressed Joe, but it made her vulnerable to the wisecracks of Jack's sisters, whom she referred to as the rah-rah girls, the family cheerleaders.

There was something overwhelming about the Kennedys. They exuded too much energy and competitiveness. They couldn't sit still and converse quietly and intelligently—they had to be playing touch football, softball, golf, or tennis, or competing in sailing regattas or swimming races, or yelling at the top of their lungs during their "debates."

There was another thing about them that also made Jacqueline frequently uncomfortable—Jack Kennedy always needed lots of people around him. Bobby, Ethel, and the rah-rah girls seemed to come constantly between her and Jack. And if it wasn't one of them, it was one or more of Jack's cronies or in-laws or political aides or former navy buddies: people like Lem Billings, Red Fay, Dave Powers, Larry O'Brien, and Kenney O'Donnell.

Despite the gregariousness of the Kennedy clan and Jack's reputation as a notorious womanizer, Jackie knew she needed to marry John F. Kennedy. Not only was she physically and emotionally attracted to him, but by marrying him she would fulfill the one great commandment of her social class: *marry well.* And marrying well meant, above all, marrying a rich man. Everyone knew the Kennedys had a lot of money. Janet Auchincloss, for whom money meant everything, was delighted with the match. Jacqueline realized, as did all the Bouviers of her generation, myself included, that the great days of the Bouvier family were long past; we would never inherit very much money from the family, and it was unlikely that any of us would ever be able to afford to live the way we did at Lasata during the 1930s and 1940s. Jackie had had it drilled into her by her mother that she had to marry well if she was going to enjoy a living standard similar to the one in which she was raised.

Of course, Jacqueline never let on in the presence of the Kennedys that she was basically poor. None of them had ever seen Lasata at the height of its splendor, but they had heard about it. Although Joe Kennedy, the Wall Street operator, must have known that M. C. Bouvier & Co. was once a very prosperous brokerage and investment banking house, he never learned that M. C.'s nephew and

heir, John V. Bouvier Jr., had dissipated much of the inherit
he had received from his uncle and left very little money to his
children and grandchildren. He was well aware of the Auchincloss
wealth, but Joe could not know that Hughdie had left Jacqueline out
of his will, favoring only his blood progeny. Jacqueline looked rich,
acted rich, and lived on two great estates, Hammersmith Farm and
Merrywood. In Joe Kennedy's estimation, she clearly was not a
gold digger, and that was a big plus in her campaign to win his
favor. In the end Jacqueline was to win over old Joe so completely
that it has been said he virtually commanded Jack to marry her.

As it would turn out, things came to a head between Jack and
Jackie in May 1953. It was then, in mid-May, that Jack Kennedy
made what Jacqueline felt was a halfhearted marriage proposal. She
promptly took off for London with her friend Aileen Bowdoin to
attend the coronation of Queen Elizabeth II and write it up for
the *Washington Times-Herald*. The trip would also give her a
breathing spell to decide whether she really wanted to marry into
the overbearing Kennedy clan. Would she lose her freedom and
identity to them? Would she be able to keep step with their enormous ambition for Jack Kennedy?

Jacqueline left suddenly, with hardly any advance notice, and
she didn't give Kennedy the impression she was going to miss him
very much. Once in London, she sent back a stream of articles to
Frank Waldrop that made the front page of the *Times-Herald* along
with letters to Jack telling him what a wonderful time she was having attending all the parties and balls and meeting so many interesting and charming men.

Among the stories she sent back were reports on Perle
Mesta's ball at Londonderry House, at which she observed Lauren
Bacall dancing with General Omar Bradley and met the attractive
young Marquess of Milford Haven, who was regarded as one of
the most eligible bachelors of the British aristocracy.

During her stay in London, Jacqueline the journalist freely
indulged in practices she was later to abhor and condemn. She

Jacqueline Bouvier, Inquiring Camera Girl for the Washington Times-Herald, *photographs a London bus driver in May 1953. She had gone to London with a friend, Aileen Bowdoin, to attend the coronation of Queen Elizabeth II and write it up for her newspaper.*

approached two nieces of Mamie Eisenhower on their way to school and wormed indiscretions out of them that enraged Mamie's sister. She also went out of her way to obtain juicy tidbits about the royal family from people who claimed they knew them. She also aggressively interviewed Elizabeth's ladies-in-waiting, an action she would recall when, ten years later, as First Lady, she forbade her ladies-in-waiting—her secretaries and assistants—to grant interviews to anyone, under pain of expulsion.

Jacqueline went to Paris for a week before returning to Washington. Just before she left, she received a telegram from the customarily undemonstrative Jack Kennedy—ARTICLES EXCELLENT BUT YOU ARE MISSED—that told Jacqueline her absence had indeed made her man's heart grow fonder.

Jacqueline Bouvier and Senator John F. Kennedy prepare to play a game of tennis at Hyannis Port, Massachusetts, on June 27, 1953, just after announcing their engagement to marry.

Not long after her return to Washington, Jacqueline accepted Jack Kennedy's marriage proposal and promptly handed in her resignation as Inquiring Camera Girl. Soon an official announcement was made. John F. Kennedy and Jacqueline Bouvier were to be formally engaged to be married on June 24, 1953, about a month before Jacqueline's twenty-fourth birthday. The wedding would take place in Newport in mid-September.

Chapter Ten

"The Wedding of the Year"

The marriage of Jacqueline Bouvier and John F. Kennedy affected many people in many different ways.

For Jack Kennedy, it meant the renunciation of his much-loved bachelorhood, the giving up, for a while at least, of the libertine ways he had reveled in all his adult existence. For Jacqueline, it meant more than giving herself up to one man; it meant surrendering to the rambunctious, clannish family that would demand considerable sacrifices of her freedom and individuality to further their ambitions.

She, of course, would be handsomely paid for those sacrifices. Finally, her money troubles would be over. She could have anything she wanted—all she had to do was send the bill to Joe Kennedy, specifically to his paymaster general at the Park Agency in New York, Thomas Walsh who paid the bills of the entire clan.

For the Kennedy family as a whole, the marriage would enhance its social position and lift them yet a few more notches above the lower-class East Boston Irish backwater from which Joseph P. Kennedy had extricated them. It would also enhance the chances of Joe Kennedy's greatest ambition: getting son Jack into the White House.

For Black Jack Bouvier, the marriage promised to wrench Jackie firmly away from the Auchinclosses, and free him from having to pay all those bills Jackie used to charge without his permission at Bloomingdale's and Saks, not to mention her $50-a-month allowance and all her medical bills from her equestrian accidents. Since he had gotten along so well with Jack Kennedy, he felt assured of being able to see Jackie regularly—or at least whenever she and Jack Kennedy would come to New York.

For the Bouvier family as a whole, the marriage would not become the crown of its history until Jacqueline eventually entered the White House. Generally speaking, the Bouviers looked down on the Kennedys as social-climbing upstarts; as arch Republicans, they were dismayed at the Kennedys' long affiliation with the Democratic Party. And, of course, no one in the family had any use for Joseph P. Kennedy, the former mob-connected bootlegger, would-be appeaser of Hitler, and the former "Judas of Wall Street," who betrayed his fellow stockbrokers by instituting regulations to ban trading practices he had once made a fortune from. I clearly remember Jack Bouvier and my father railing against Joe Kennedy on numerous occasions, calling him an opportunist, a traitor, and a crook.

As for the Auchinclosses, who, because of their proximity to the John F. Kennedys in Washington during the winter and in Newport during the summer, saw a good deal more of the couple, they came to enjoy a measure of what Gore Vidal, their erstwhile stepson, has termed RG—Reflected Glory. Hughdie, it appears, especially savored this status. He would be gratified to know that Hammersmith Farm, which eventually had to be sold by Janet in 1977, a year after his death, for only $850,000 to pay off the debts of his estate (the firm of Auchincloss, Redpath, and Parker had gone under), would become a museum called Camelot Gardens and be billed as President Kennedy's "Summer White House." But Hughdie doubtless would have had mixed feelings about the 1995 asking price of Camelot Gardens: $9,500,000.

Janet was delighted with the marriage. The Kennedys were just the sort of big game she had been after for Jackie—the "real money" she counseled her daughters to go for.

As for Jackie's maternal grandfather James T. Lee, the marriage would destroy their relationship permanently. We don't know precisely why, but Lee so detested Joseph P. Kennedy that he told Jackie that if she married his son he would never speak to her again. Was it politics that came between the two multimillionaires—Lee was an ardent Republican—or something else? My father thought it was over money, business. Both men were shrewd real-estate investors who had made fortunes buying and selling commercial and residential real estate. Perhaps they had had acrimonious business dealings. If the John F. Kennedy Library in Boston ever gets around to disgorging the financial records of Joseph P. Kennedy from 1920 to 1960, which are not yet open to the public, we may finally know.

Old Man Lee did not attend John F. Kennedy's inauguration, nor did he ever visit his granddaughter in the White House. And, although Janet approved of the marriage, I do not believe she was ever comfortable with the Kennedys or took any particular pride in Jackie when she became First Lady. Having no sense of history, and little education, she felt that being the mother of the First Lady was something of a nuisance, bringing more aggravations than satisfactions.

The major beneficiaries of the marriage of Jacqueline Bouvier to John F. Kennedy were the American people. It gave them a breath of fresh air, and presented them with an exciting new image of a politician and his wife who were young, attractive, articulate, and had a unique sense of style, at least for American politicians. The Bouvier-Kennedy marriage was destined to give the American people a short-lived, incandescent, and ultimately tragic and majestic moment they would never forget—and never come close to experiencing again.

On June 24, the Hugh D. Auchinclosses held an engagement party at Hammersmith Farm for Jacqueline and Jack, and an official announcement of their engagement was sent to the press. On hand were an assortment of Auchinclosses, Kennedys, and a few friends. Jack Bouvier had pointedly not been invited, and he was deeply offended by the snub. By then Jacqueline had become a captive of the Auchinclosses and the Kennedys and had no say in the matter. She would gradually learn that she would have to acquiesce to practically everything the Kennedys demanded from her in their inexorable pursuit of the White House.

By June 24, Jack Bouvier had already been working on his tan on weekends in East Hampton, where he had rented a cottage for the summer. For hours on end, he would soak up the sun on the beach or in the men's solarium at the Maidstone Club. Still trim and handsome at sixty-two, with his jet black hair intact except for a splash of silver at his temples, he had planned to cut a dashing figure at Jackie's engagement party. Now he would have to wait for the main event on September 12, when he would give Jackie away to her groom in style.

Planning well ahead, Black Jack visited his tailor, Tripler's in New York, to get fitted for the cutaway he was going to wear at Jackie's wedding. The seamstresses and stitchers needed plenty of time to make all the inevitable alterations, for Jack Bouvier was a very fastidious dresser who never bought a suit off the rack in his life.

Meanwhile, at a party given to celebrate the Bouvier-Kennedy engagement in Hyannis Port, two young men in three-piece suits arrived from Van Cleef & Arpels, one of New York's premier jewelers, to deliver Jackie's engagement ring. It was a magnificent emerald-and-diamond creation that Jack Kennedy had casually charged to the Park Agency. Jackie was, of course, thrilled as Jack placed the ring on her finger. Think what clothes and jewels lay ahead.

The next day, Jack Kennedy was on the phone most of the morning with his secretary, Evelyn Lincoln, reeling off scores of names for wedding invitations. Although he had assured Janet and Jacqueline that he was going to invite only close friends, the list he dictated to Evelyn Lincoln included practically the entire Senate as well as every Democratic politician in Massachusetts. During the rest of July, Jack and Jackie went over the invitation list endlessly

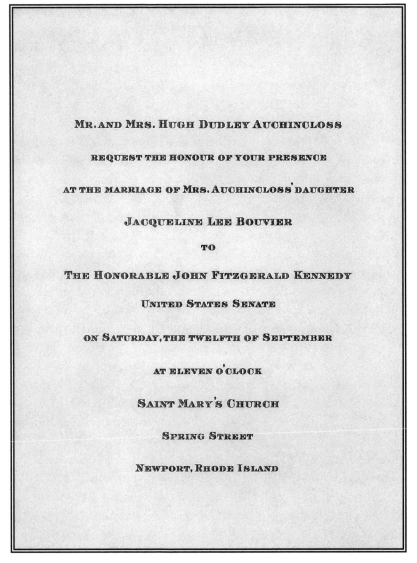

MR. AND MRS. HUGH DUDLEY AUCHINCLOSS

REQUEST THE HONOUR OF YOUR PRESENCE

AT THE MARRIAGE OF MRS. AUCHINCLOSS' DAUGHTER

JACQUELINE LEE BOUVIER

TO

THE HONORABLE JOHN FITZGERALD KENNEDY

UNITED STATES SENATE

ON SATURDAY, THE TWELFTH OF SEPTEMBER

AT ELEVEN O'CLOCK

SAINT MARY'S CHURCH

SPRING STREET

NEWPORT, RHODE ISLAND

The invitation to the wedding of Jacqueline Bouvier and John F. Kennedy. More than seven hundred people were invited.

and, it is believed, not without some friction. Jacqueline, after all, had her own constituency to invite: the entire Bouvier family, all the vast tribe of Auchinclosses, those members of the Lee family willing to incur the displeasure of Old Man Lee, all Jackie's school and college mates at Miss Porter's, Vassar, La Sorbonne, and George Washington. By the end of the month the long list was complete.

After Congress adjourned in early August, Jack Kennedy did something that profoundly shocked his young bride-to-be. He abruptly took off for a last fling in Europe with his former Harvard roommate, Torbert "Torby" Macdonald, leaving Jackie to cope with all the wedding preparations without his support and advice. Jack and Torby chartered a yacht in Cannes and cruised the Riviera, picking up women in Juan Les Pins, Nice, and Antibes. It was typical Kennedy. The prospect of settling down to marriage with only one sexual partner made him terribly uncomfortable.

Jacqueline was not the only person shocked by Kennedy's abrupt last fling, which, of course, was far from his last. Janet was also very disturbed by it. She told Jackie and Hughdie and many others that a man who was really in love with a woman would not leave her a few weeks before their marriage to dally with girls in bikinis who loll around the beaches of the French Riviera.

How did Jacqueline cope with Jack Kennedy's reputation as a notorious womanizer? How did she deal with the virtual certainty that Kennedy would betray her sexually? Again, I believe that her experience with her "dangerous" father had taught her that "all men are unfaithful" and that she would simply have to accept the fact that her "dangerous" husband would have many extramarital affairs. Eventually she would even become flippant about it. After she learned that one of her secretaries, Pamela Turnure, was having an affair with the President, one day, she was taking a French photographer on a tour of the White House and, as she opened an office door and spotted Pam Turnure at a desk inside, told the photographer in French: "And this is a young lady who is supposed to be sleeping with my husband."

In the weeks before her marriage, Jackie was both perplexed and apprehensive about her impending union. She also knew that, besides being a womanizer, Jack very much enjoyed being with his old buddies, guys like Red Fay, Torby Macdonald, Lemoyne Billings (who would one day have his own room in the White House), Larry O'Brien, and Dave Powers. What was she going to do when she wanted him all to herself?

I believe that Jackie answered these questions by deceiving herself. Self-deception—in her case, a form of wishful thinking— was the way she coped with the more unpleasant realities of her life. For years she had denied to herself and others that there was any trouble between Mummy and Daddy, when everyone knew there was deep trouble. For years she would turn a blind eye to Jack Kennedy's innumerable infidelities, telling herself that they never happened, or, that if they did, they were utterly inconsequential. As she once told Joan Kennedy, "Kennedy men are like that. They'll go after anything in skirts. It doesn't mean a thing."

Eventually Jack and Torby returned from their fling on the Riviera, and the planning for what the press had already billed as "The Wedding of the Year" picked up steam. First would come the prenuptial festivities: two bachelor dinners, a succession of luncheons and teas, and a big bridal dinner at Newport.

While Kennedy and his Harvard buddy were playing the field, and Jacqueline was fretting about him as she went about her wedding preparations, Jack Bouvier was doing his own planning in New York and East Hampton for the biggest role in his life— father of the bride at the Wedding of the Year.

On three-day weekends in East Hampton, he had taken to jogging along the ocean at the Maidstone beach, a form of exercise he was not accustomed to. He wanted to look as fit as possible for Jackie's wedding, and after his run and a swim he would lie under the blazing August sun for a couple of hours, his face glistening with oil, working on his ever-deepening tan. He was polishing his movie-star image. He knew that a deep tan against a starched white shirt collar would enhance his legendary Clark Gable–Rhett Butler look.

During the week in New York he visited Tripler's regularly. He wanted his cutaway to be immaculately tailored. He took great care over such details as the width of his lapels and the length of his sleeves. Jack, like many Mediterranean men, liked to shoot plenty of gleaming white linen and preferred to keep his jacket lapels low around his neck and his jacket sleeves somewhat shorter than is usually the fashion. He was also very careful about the width and length of his trousers. They had to be relatively narrow and break ever so slightly over his highly polished black shoes.

To complete his outfit, he was being fitted with a gray waistcoat that would come down just far enough beneath the lapels of his cutaway; he would also be wearing new gray suede gloves and a precious heirloom, his grand-uncle M. C. Bouvier's diamond-and-pearl stickpin, which had been in the family over a hundred years.

Yes, when he eventually reached Newport and took his beloved Jacqueline down the aisle of St. Mary's he was going to show the world—the press, Newport society, the Auchinclosses, the Kennedys, Uncle Hughdie, Joe Kennedy, and Janet—just who Jackie's *real* father was.

While Jack Bouvier was making his preparations, plans for all the prenuptial events in Newport and Hyannis were unfolding at a rapid pace and secretaries were frantically sending out invitations.

For Jack Kennedy, his wedding had become just as much a political campaign as a family event. There were myriad events: a big bachelor dinner in Boston financed by Joe Kennedy ten days before the wedding, a weekend-long house party at the Kennedy compound at Hyannis Port for the ten bridesmaids and fourteen ushers, another bachelor dinner to be given by Hughdie at Newport's Clambake Club, and a huge bridal dinner the night before the wedding, also at the Clambake Club, hosted by Ambassador and Mrs. Joseph P. Kennedy.

Alone in his drab bachelor quarters at 125 East 74th Street, with no other company but his faithful maid Esther, who had worked for the Bouvier family for over twenty years, Jack Bouvier waited and waited for the invitations to these events. They never came. He knew about them, for he kept in touch with my mother and her twin who reluctantly told him what was going on in Newport and Hyannis. (They and their husbands had been invited to everything.) It is not known whether Jackie was in touch with him during this frantic and anxious period, but it was believed that, contrary to her instincts and wishes, she was not. Janet was keeping close watch on her daughter, and since she did not want Jack Bouvier to give her away, we can be sure she monitored Jackie's telephone calls closely. According to my father, Jack often looked despondent when he arrived at his Wall Street office in the morning. It seemed to him that his exclusion from the prenuptial festivities in Newport and Hyannis had made him lose his zest for in-and-out trading.

Not even Lee was much of a solace to Jack during the weeks preceding Jacqueline's marriage. She and her husband, Michael Canfield, were living fairly close to Jack, at 14 Sutton Place South, but there appears to have been relatively little contact between them. It is my guess that Janet told her younger daughter to keep her distance from her father as part of her campaign to prevent Jack from giving Jackie away at the impending wedding.

Jack had not expected to be asked to the big bachelor dinner given by Joe Kennedy in Boston to which mostly Massachusetts politicians had been invited, but he had half hoped to go to the intimate bachelor dinner in Newport, even though it was hosted by Hughdie; he definitely expected to be invited to the big bridal dinner the night before the wedding. After all, he *was* the father of the bride, a bride he had brought up, educated, and supported for twenty-four years, and he had every right to be accorded a place of honor at these celebrations.

What Jack should have realized, but didn't, was that Janet Auchincloss was dead set on excluding him from everything. Her reason had nothing to do with their marital squabbles of eighteen years ago. The reason, I believe, was pure jealousy. Janet was insanely jealous of her daughters' love for their father, their *prefer-ence* for him over her.

If Janet could have summoned the moral courage, she would have excluded *all* the Bouviers from Jacqueline's wedding. At the time of her separation and divorce, she had felt the entire Bouvier family had been arrayed against her, which it had. I well remember how Jack's older sister, Big Edie, used to taunt and ridicule her. But Janet did not have the courage not to invite Jack's younger sisters, Maude and Michelle, and their husbands and children. The twins had been Janet's closest friends when she was a young girl— after all, they had introduced her to their brother.

The fundamental problem between Jack and Janet had been Janet's inability to *control* Jack; she could neither boss him around nor prevent her daughters from loving their father more than her.

What the twins had noted at Merrywood during the wedding reception for Lee Bouvier and Michael Canfield was Janet's control of Hughdie Auchincloss. Although he was a tall man with an imposing physique and was very rich, Janet led him around by the nose, treating him like a servant. "Hughdie, do this." "Hughdie, take care of that." She and Lee clearly had the upper hand.

When the twins arrived in Newport in September 1953, they noticed the same situation. Janet was in total charge. Hughdie followed her like some huge hound dog.

What Janet had done was to assume control of all the arrangements for the prenuptial celebrations not already appropriated by Joe Kennedy. She took complete charge of the bride's half of the invitation lists and of all the seating at the various parties, pointedly excluding her ex-husband.

The first bachelor party, to which Jack Bouvier knew he would not be invited, was held on September 2. It was more of a political event and, in fact, had been staged by Joe Kennedy to promote his son as a rising star in the Democratic party. About 350 men had been invited, including Kennedy's campaign chairmen from every section of Massachusetts, many of Jack's old school, college, and navy buddies, and, of course, the press. The bachelor dinner was given at Boston's Parker House. One of the principal speakers was Jack Kennedy's twenty-eight-year-old kid brother Bobby, who was so nervous and shy, according to Jack's old navy buddy, Red Fay, that his hands "quivered" and his voice "quaked." Bobby, at that stage of his life, was in awe of his big brother, Senator Jack.

The second bachelor dinner was a small, black-tie affair at Newport's Clambake Club hosted by Hugh D. Auchincloss for close male friends and relatives of Jack and Jacqueline. The party and the names of all the guests were somehow leaked to the press and written up in the New York papers, so Jack had to endure being the butt of countless jokes of his fellow brokers who wanted him to explain why the father of the bride wasn't at fellow stock-broker Hugh Auchincloss's bachelor dinner. "Taking another loss with Auchincloss, Jack?" they taunted him.

As the bridal dinner approached, Jack Bouvier packed his bags and traveled to Newport, where he put up at the Viking Hotel. His twin sisters had already checked into the Hotel Munchener King. On arriving at the Viking, Jack telephoned Jacqueline at Hammersmith Farm to let her know he was now in Newport and eagerly awaiting the festivities. The twins also called Jacqueline and found her in high spirits. They made no mention of her father. The next day Ambassador and Mrs. Joseph P. Kennedy were to host the bridal dinner at the Clambake Club for the bridal couple and their families and the fourteen ushers and ten bridesmaids.

Jack Bouvier remained at the Viking Hotel, where, as the father of the bride in Newport's biggest wedding in years, he was treated like a king. He spent his time making sure his wardrobe would be in perfect shape, that his cutaway and trousers would be sharply pressed, his shoes immaculately shined. Then he waited for his invitation to the bridal dinner. What went on over the tele-phone between the Viking Hotel and Hammersmith Farm during this period is not known. What we know is that Jack Bouvier was not invited to the bridal dinner and it crushed him. He was not even given a chance to see Jackie the day before her wedding. Janet had her secretary screen all incoming calls: "No, Miss Bouvier is not available at the moment." "No, I'm sorry but Mrs. Auchincloss has gone out for a while." "No, I don't know when she'll be back." Beyond these few scraps, nothing more is known.

We can be sure, however, that Jack Bouvier went to bed that night deeply offended.

While Jack Bouvier was nursing his wounds at the Viking Hotel, Joe Kennedy's guests at the bridal dinner were having a riotous time at the Clambake Club. Jack Kennedy gave his fourteen ushers monogrammed Brooks Brothers umbrellas, and Jackie presented her bridesmaids with monogrammed silver picture frames. The toasts were short and teasing. The bridegroom told everyone that the real reason he was marrying Jackie was to silence her. Her Inquiring Camera Girl columns in the *Washington Times-Herald* were beginning to menace his political career. Jackie then countered by telling the bridal party what a flop Jack had been as a suitor. During their entire courtship, Kennedy, who prided himself on his command of the English language, had not written her a single amorous letter, only one postcard from Bermuda. She then held it up for all to see, and read aloud: "Dear Jackie, Wish you were here. Jack."

September 12, 1953, turned out to be an almost perfect day. A clear sky. A blazing sun. Not too hot, not too cool. But it was very windy, as Newport is apt to be as fall approaches. As a result, the women had to hold onto their wide-brimmed hats and the men encountered trouble keeping their hair from standing on end.

The marriage ceremony was essentially a creation of Joseph P. Kennedy, whose principal aim was to put on a spectacle that would place his son Jack in the spotlight of national attention. In addition to the Bouviers, Auchinclosses, Kennedys, and their friends, he made sure there would be many influential members of the Fourth Estate in the congregation, especially political commentators and reporters for such national magazines as *Time* and *Newsweek*. He had also made sure that invitations had been sent to the most powerful syndicated columnists, film celebrities, congressmen, and even the Speaker of the House.

Although Joe Kennedy was hardly a very religious man, he prided himself on being an ardent Catholic; he had cultivated high-ranking Catholic clergymen all his life. They could be powerful political allies. It was through his auspices, then, that he enlisted the archbishop of Boston, Richard Cushing, to celebrate the high nuptial mass at St. Mary's, assisted by Monsignor Francis Rossiter and three other prominent Catholic clergymen—Bishop Weldon of Springfield, the Very Reverend John Cavanagh, former president of Notre Dame, and the Reverend James Keller of New York, leader of the influential Christopher movement. To complete this nuptial extravaganza, he persuaded the famous tenor, Luigi Vena, to sing the "Ave Maria" and made arrangements with the Vatican for the bride and groom to receive the Apostolic Blessing of Pope Pius XII.

Jacqueline's mood at Hammersmith Farm as she dressed for the most important day of her life can only be guessed at. I never discussed it with her, nor did I ever mention to her the tragic scenes at the Viking Hotel with Jack Bouvier raving against the Auchinclosses and Joe Kennedy to my father. The subject of Jacqueline's wedding and Janet's preventing her daughter from being given away by her father at the ceremony would be forever verboten in Jacqueline's presence. So deeply distressing was this episode to all concerned that even today, over forty years later, with all the principals in the drama now dead, my mother, the sole survivor and witness to the heartrending behind-the-scenes events of "The Wedding of the Year," still cannot discuss it.

Jacqueline was dressing for her wedding to John F. Kennedy without knowing whether her stepfather, Hughdie Auchincloss, whom she respected, or her father, whom she dearly loved, would take her down the aisle of St. Mary's to her destiny. Jackie wanted very much to be given away by her real father. But her strong-willed mother would not countenance that. She wanted her daughter to be given away by Hugh D. Auchincloss.

While Jack Bouvier was dressing for the wedding, Maude and Michelle and their husbands, John E. Davis and Harrington Putnam, were busily getting themselves ready. The plan was for my father and Mr. Putnam, known to the family as Put, to pick Jack up at the Viking, take him to the Munchener King to get the twins, and then have all five proceed to St. Mary's to join Janet, Jacqueline, and Archbishop Cushing in the church vestibule.

When my father and Uncle Put arrived in Jack Bouvier's room, they found the father of the bride in a very tense, fighting mood. He had endured two devastating snubs from Janet and the Auchinclosses on two successive evenings. He adored his daughter Jacqueline and wanted so desperately to give her away in style and make her proud of him. Yet the wedding ceremony and the reception at Hammersmith Farm had been organized by his hated rivals, the Auchinclosses, and the Judas who had ruined his business, Joseph P. Kennedy. Thus, he was confronted with a situation so emotionally explosive he dared not dwell on it too long. Fortunately, his two brothers-in-law were on hand to lend him moral support.

My father and Uncle Put soon realized Jack needed all the moral support he could get. They found him only half-dressed and in a state of extreme confusion. He had already put on his shirt and striped trousers and his gray double-breasted vest, but had not yet gotten around to his tie or cutaway or shoes—and he was due at St. Mary's within a half hour. On the dresser they spotted a tray with the remains of a half-eaten breakfast of scrambled eggs, bacon, toast, and coffee. They also noticed a bucket full of ice, a bottle of scotch, and half a glass of scotch and water.

To my father and Harrington Putnam, Jack looked agitated but eminently sober as he told his brothers-in-law that he was feeling great and looking forward to the wedding. As my father and Uncle Put were assessing his physical condition and state of readiness, my mother and her twin were putting the last touches on their outfits, and the calls began coming through to the twins from Hammersmith Farm.

Janet wanted to know from Michelle if Jack Bouvier was "all right."

Jackie asked my mother if Daddy was "up to it."

The twins replied that they didn't know yet. Their husbands had just gone over to the Viking "to help Jack get dressed."

From the tone of Janet's and Jackie's voices, the twins concluded that the mood at Hammersmith Farm was close to hysteria. Perhaps, they suggested, they would have to get Hughdie as a substitute if Jack couldn't pull himself together. In what would be the first of many such times, Jacqueline found herself torn between the demands of the Kennedys' thirst for publicity and her own personal emotions—in this case her deep love for her father.

As she later told him in a moving letter, she wanted so much for him to give her away, but she was not allowed to by her mother and Joe Kennedy. What she didn't mention was that she also had to contend with all those reporters, gossip columnists, political commentators, and photographers Joe Kennedy had invited to the wedding. Could she take the risk of having a Jack Bouvier on her arm who couldn't walk a straight line down the center aisle of St. Mary's? Wouldn't it be far safer, for publicity purposes, to have Uncle Hughdie guide her down the aisle?

While Jacqueline was putting the finishing touches on her wedding outfit—a taffeta faille gown, creamy white to blend with the faintly yellow rose-point lace veil lent by Janet's mother—my father and Harrington Putnam were attempting to gauge Jack Bouvier's condition. They noticed Jack drain his highball as he tried to work his tie into his high, stiff collar. Then he couldn't find his stickpin. Soon he was going over to the ice bucket to prepare another drink.

In contrast with the tense preparations at Hammersmith Farm and the Viking Hotel, Senator John F. Kennedy was dressing calmly. Kennedy, who usually functioned best in a crisis, was looking forward to basking in the spotlight. If the wedding photographs turned out as well as he hoped, the wedding could land him and Jackie on a few front pages and even some magazine covers. They had already graced the cover of *Life* magazine after their engagement was announced. Hughdie Auchincloss had put two of Hammersmith Farm's spacious guesthouses at the Kennedys' disposal. From all accounts, not only Jack but Father Joe and Mother Rose were in an upbeat mood, and so were Bobby and Teddy and the girls. They were all looking forward to a great day, one that could conceivably lend impetus to Jack's inevitable march to the White House.

In the Bouvier-Auchincloss camps, tension was mounting. Feeling under great pressure, my father and Harrington Putnam were trying to decide whether Jack Bouvier was fit to perform his duties. They concluded that, although he had had a few drinks, he was by no means drunk and could, in all probability, guide Jackie down the aisle. As a precaution, Harrington Putnam took the bottle of scotch off Jack's dresser while Jack was hunting for his stickpin, and hid it in the closet.

My mother and my aunt continued to be assailed by hysterical calls from Hammersmith Farm. Janet demanded to know if Jack Bouvier had been drinking. My mother tried to minimize the situation; she conceded that my father had told her that Jack had had "one or two sips" but was okay. He was by no means intoxicated; he was steady on his feet and in a good mood.

"I don't care," snapped Janet. "We don't want him at the wedding even if he had only a couple of *sips.*"

"But John and Put believe he can perform," my mother emphasized.

"I don't care," cried Janet, "Don't dare bring him. If you do, Jackie and I will never speak to you again."

"I'll call the Viking again to see what's going on," my mother said and hung up.

Matters had now reached a critical stage for all concerned. Jack Bouvier, who had almost completed dressing, began to rail against Janet and the Auchinclosses for how they had excluded him from all the prenuptial events, especially the small bachelor dinner given for members of the family and the ushers and bridesmaids. This was an ominous sign, but it did not faze my father. He had spent half his adult life listening to Jack Bouvier rail against Janet and the Auchinclosses.

Soon Jack was fully dressed, and my father later told me he looked splendid in his immaculately tailored, beautifully fitted cutaway and deep East Hampton tan. Although his tongue was a little thick, he was coherent and both physically and mentally up to the duties he was to perform at St. Mary's. My father phoned this opinion to my mother at the Munchener King, who, in turn, relayed it to Janet at Hammersmith Farm, with Michelle seconding her opinion.

Janet would hear none of it. Hugh was now dressed and ready to give Jackie away. They were all losing time and before long they would have to leave for St. Mary's. The limousine was already parked outside the front door with its engine running. If the twins brought Jack Bouvier with them, Janet would not let them in the church door and there might be a scene. "Keep him there," Janet urged with that strident voice of hers. "Don't let him out of his room . . . even for *one second*."

The twins had no choice but to accede to Janet's wishes. They phoned the Viking and told their husbands to prevent Jack from leaving his room. Both my father and Harrington Putnam remonstrated, insisting that Jack was in good shape. After a heated argument, the two men gave in and so my father and Uncle Put, reduced to being Jack Bouvier's guardians, missed both the wedding and the big reception at Hammersmith Farm.

Janet had won. She now had the wedding the way *she* had wanted it, with her husband, Hugh D. Auchincloss, taking her daughter down the center aisle. Jackie was, of course, deeply disappointed and very worried about her father. But she could do nothing; Jackie was no longer her own master. She had become an unwilling pawn of her mother's animosity toward Jack Bouvier and, more important, was already a tool, an instrument, of the Kennedys' relentless political machine. From now on, she had no choice but to do what was beneficial for the Kennedy image.

Now, after the turmoil and disappointments of the past hour and a half, Jacqueline summoned her emotional strength and rose to the occasion. Triumphing over the tensions, and sadness, of the morning, she appeared a poised, smiling bride to the 600 invited guests cramming St. Mary's and the 3,000 spectators who lined the avenue leading to the church.

Hugh D. Auchincloss took his stepdaughter's arm as she

Jacqueline Bouvier and her stepfather, Hugh D. Auchincloss, arrive at St. Mary's Church in Newport, Rhode Island, for her wedding to Senator John F. Kennedy, September 12, 1953. The bride's mother, Janet, who had prevented Jack Bouvier from giving his daughter away, is to the left, looking triumphant.

entered the church. The tall, solid Newport patrician then performed his role with calm dignity as he guided Jacqueline down the center aisle, followed by the matron of honor, Lee Canfield, and her bridesmaids.

As Jacqueline made her way toward the altar and her bridegroom, she radiated a serene beauty that captivated the congregation. Very few people, only members of the Bouvier family and their friends, noted that she was not on the arm of her father. As she walked past the front pews, her twin aunts burst into tears as they recalled the high drama of the past two hours and the

Jacqueline Bouvier and John F. Kennedy, now man and wife, leave St. Mary's Church in Newport, September 12, 1953, after what the press billed as "The Wedding of the Year."

pathetic spectacle of their brother being held captive at the Viking by their husbands.

Although Jacqueline's wedding to John F. Kennedy received an immense amount of press attention throughout the nation, not many people had the remotest idea of what the bride had gone through that morning. In her first few minutes as a Kennedy, she had not only risen to the occasion, knowing she was being married before the eyes of the nation, but had done so under the most distressing circumstances imaginable. The radiance she exuded came from deep reserves of emotional strength—those reserves she had displayed since childhood, when, as a girl of only five, she summoned the will to win first prize in her class at the East Hampton horse show.

Jacqueline Bouvier Kennedy and her husband, Senator John F. Kennedy, on the lawn of the Auchincloss estate, Hammersmith Farm, on their wedding day, September 12, 1953.

Jacqueline Bouvier Kennedy, on the main staircase of Hammersmith Farm, prepares to toss her bridal bouquet to her bridesmaids below after her wedding reception at the Auchincloss estate, September 12, 1953.

From now on, Jacqueline's life would be a continuous succession of rising to great occasions, a series of rehearsals, as it would turn out, for that one momentous occasion, when, on November 25, 1963, before the eyes of the entire world, she performed her last wifely duty to John F. Kennedy.

Acknowledgments

This book is principally a product of my memory, and, as such, is partly autobiographical. However, I could not rely wholly on my memory, and wish to acknowledge the contributions of others.

I would first like to acknowledge, with much gratitude, the research done on the Bouvier family's ancestry in France by Yves Chassin du Guerny of Nîmes and the pioneer research done on Michel Bouvier's early career in Philadelphia by Francis J. Dallett of the American Museum of Britain and by Mary Vespa of *Colonial Homes* magazine. Next I would like to thank various members of the Bouvier family, notably my cousins Michelle "Shella" Crouse and the late Michel Bouvier III, for their anecdotes about Jacqueline Bouvier's youth and adolescence. My principal debt of gratitude goes to my mother, Maude Bouvier Davis, who saved the Bouvier family papers and memorabilia—letters, photographs, wills, diaries, notes, and so on—from destruction and turned them all over to me.

I am also deeply indebted to my editor at John Wiley & Sons, Hana Umlauf Lane, who commissioned this book and whose judicious editing of the manuscript improved it significantly. My thanks also go to her courteous and efficient editorial assistant, Lis Cobas, with whom it was always a pleasure to do business, to

Rosemary Wellner for her thorough copyediting, and to my agent, Marianne Strong, who first introduced me to John Wiley & Sons. I wish also to thank my word processor, Carol Deacon, of Soho Word Pro, for her efficient and punctual preparation of the manuscript.

Photo Credits

Grateful acknowledgment is made to the following for permission to reproduce the photographs used in this book. Every reasonable effort has been made to contact the copyright holders of material used here. Omissions brought to our attention will be corrected in future editions.

Frontispiece (facing Contents)—Sygma; pp. 18, 22 (both), 28, 30, 41, 83, 86, 99, 101, 174, 196, 197—Molly Thayer Collection/ Magnum Photos; pp. 31 and 34—UPI/Bettmann; pp. 32, 40, 77, 110—courtesy of Kathleen Bouvier; p. 80—courtesy of East Hampton Library, Long Island Collection. Originally appeared in *The Social Spectator,* August 30, 1941; pp. 103 and 104—Robert Meservey/Magnum Photos.

Index

Aldrich, Winthrop, 168

Anderson, Bernice, 59–60, 64–65

Appaquoque House. *See* Wildmoor (East Hampton home)

Auchincloss, Hugh D. III "Yusha" (stepbrother), 82, 89, 122, 138, 139

Auchincloss, Hugh D. Jr. "Hughdie" (stepfather)
  background of, 80, 82
  and family fortune, 80, 82, 173
  gives JB away at wedding, 193–194
  helps JB get job with *Washington Times-Herald,* 158
  hosts prenuptial parties for JB and John F. Kennedy, 179–180, 187
  marries Janet Lee Bouvier, 80, 82

Auchincloss, James Lee (half-brother), 82, 102

Auchincloss, Janet Jennings (half-sister), 82, 97

Auchincloss, Janet Lee (mother)
  aftermath of divorce from Jack Bouvier, 79–80
  birth of Caroline Lee, 26
  birth of Jacqueline, 17
  birth of James Lee Auchincloss, 82, 102
  birth of Janet Jennings Auchincloss, 82, 97
  described, 25–26, 43, 186
  and JB's wedding, 182, 185–186, 187, 190–191, 192, 193
  marries Hugh Auchincloss, 80, 82, 113
  marries Jack Bouvier, 21, 23, 24–26

  relationship with JB, 26, 47, 49–50, 135, 144–146
  rivalry over JB's affection, 87, 89, 96–97, 123, 124, 141–142
  sues Jack Bouvier for divorce, 70–71, 73, 74
  trains JB as equestrienne, 26, 47
  unhappiness in marriage to Jack Bouvier, 42, 47–52, 55–58, 59, 63–71
  view of daughter's marriage to John F. Kennedy, 178, 179

Auchincloss, Nina Gore Vidal. *See* Vidal, Nina Gore

Auchincloss, Nina (stepsister), 82

Auchincloss, Redpath, and Parker (firm), 82

Auchincloss, Thomas (stepbrother), 82

Auchincloss family
  background of, 80, 82, 125–126
  view of Kennedy family, 178

Bailey's Beach (Newport), 128, 130

Bartlett, Charles and Martha, 159

Beale, Bouvier (cousin), 17, 93

Beale, Edith Bouvier "Big Edie" (aunt)
  birth of, 3
  and family fortune, 112
  and Grey Gardens, 8, 44, 136, 163
  as singer, 9, 44, 62, 63, 75, 130
  unconventionality of, 7–8, 46, 57, 186

Beale, Edith "Little Edie" (cousin), 8, 17, 44, 55, 95, 163

Beale, Phelan (cousin), 8, 17, 93

Bellport (home), 59, 64, 65

Berenson, Bernard, 152–154, 157

Billings, Lemoyne, 172, 183
Bissell, Julia, 114
Black Jack Bouvier. *See* Bouvier, John
    Vernou III "Black Jack" (father)
Bonaparte, Joseph, 1, 12, 33, 130
Bonaparte, Napoleon, 1, 119, 130
Bouvier, Caroline Ewing (great-
    grandmother), 23
Bouvier, Caroline "Lee" (sister)
    and Bernard Berenson, 152–154, 157
    birth of, 26
    career of, 168
    and family fortune, 168
    graduation trip to Europe, 152–155
    and JB's wedding, 185, 194
    marries Michael Canfield, 164,
        168–169, 185
    named Debutante of the Year, 168
    and *One Special Summer,* 27, 155
    public image of, 155
    relationship with father, 61, 116,
        117, 185
    rivalry with JB, 26, 168
    at Sarah Lawrence College, 155, 157
    view of father, 166
Bouvier, Edith. *See* Beale, Edith
    Bouvier "Big Edie" (aunt)
Bouvier, Emma. *See* Drexel, Emma
    Bouvier (great-great-aunt)
Bouvier, Jacqueline Lee
    acquiescence to Kennedys, 182, 193
    aftermath of *Vogue* competition,
        151–152, 158
    becomes part of Auchincloss family,
        82, 84
    birth of, 17
    and Bouvier cousins, 17, 21, 39, 55
    christening of, 20–21
    coming-out parties, 102–104, 106
    and decorating, 116
    described, 27, 60, 78, 89, 91–92, 93,
        94, 95, 120–121, 162–162
    describes self for *Vogue* competition,
        144–146
    development of tastes, 30, 33, 37, 39
    divided world of, 91, 102, 106

engagement to John F. Kennedy, 176
as equestrienne, 14–15, 26, 28, 39,
    42, 47, 54–55, 75, 77–78, 92, 158
and family fortune, 112, 138, 173
and father's absence from her
    wedding, 189, 191, 193
graduates from Miss Porter's School,
    100–102
graduates from George Washington
    University, 152
graduation trip to Europe, 152–155
influence of Bouvier grandparents,
    33–34
interests of, 39, 42, 47, 116
job at *Washington Times-Herald,*
    158–159, 160, 161, 162, 163,
    173–174
Junior Year Abroad at Sorbonne,
    119, 123, 130–136, 138–139, 146
maternal instincts, 97
meets John F. Kennedy, 159
at Miss Chapin's School, 28, 30, 71
at Miss Porter's School, 95–96,
    100–102
money issues, 112–114, 122–123,
    138, 172–173, 177
named Debutante of the Year,
    107–109
and need to marry well, 113, 114,
    138, 172–173, 177
in Nevada, 73–74
and *One Special Summer,* 27, 95, 96,
    152–155
parental rivalry for her affection,
    58–60, 87, 89, 123, 124, 141–142
and parents' problems, 42, 49–50,
    52–53, 60, 71, 73–74, 78
preference for adults, 76, 92
public image of, 155
relationships with men, 39, 108,
    109, 114, 121–122, 135–136,
    138, 182, 183
relationship with father, 49, 50, 74,
    76–77, 87, 89, 96, 115, 116,
    123–124, 130–131, 132, 134–135,
    157, 158, 166

relationship with Hugh Auchincloss,
84
relationship with John F. Kennedy,
138, 158, 160–168, 170,
171–174, 176, 177, 182–183
relationship with John G. W.
Husted, 114, 159
relationship with Joseph P. Kennedy,
170, 171–173
relationship with mother, 26, 47,
49–50, 135, 144–146
resemblance to father, 21
secretive nature of, 53–54, 78, 89
spending habits of, 122–123
as student, 52, 58, 96
summers in East Hampton, 14–15,
33, 43–44, 46–47, 59–64, 75–76,
85, 91–95, 98, 100, 128–130,
138, 139
travels in Europe, 116–117, 119,
130–132, 152–155
and Vassar, 107, 119–121, 124
view of marriage to John Kennedy,
177
and *Vogue* magazine Prix de Paris
competition, 142–144, 146–151
voice of, 95, 128
wedding to John F. Kennedy,
177–195
Bouvier, Janet Lee. *See* Auchincloss,
Janet Lee (mother)
Bouvier, John Vernou III "Black Jack"
(father)
and Anne Plugge, 85, 87, 95,
133–134
in Army Signal Corps, 9
birth of, 3
courtship of Janet Lee, 50–51
described, 23, 43, 96
inheritance from father, 112
and JB's prenuptial events, 184, 185,
186–187
and JB's wedding, 180, 183–184,
187, 189–190, 191, 192–193
at Lee Bouvier's wedding, 169–170
marries Janet Lee, 21, 23, 24–26

meets John F. Kennedy, 164,
166–167
relationship with daughters, 58–62,
65, 75, 76–77, 87, 89, 115, 116,
117, 164, 166, 185
relationship with JB, 49, 50, 74,
76–77, 87, 89, 96, 115, 116,
123–124, 130–131, 132, 134–135,
157, 158, 166
rivalry over JB's affection, 87, 89,
96–97, 123, 124, 141–142
and stock market crash, 20
sued for divorce, 70–71, 73, 74
unhappiness in marriage, 42, 47–52,
55–58, 63–71
view of daughter's marriage to John
Kennedy, 178
view of Hugh Auchincloss, 84
view of Joseph P. Kennedy, 166, 178
as womanizer, 47–49, 66–71, 76
as youth, 5, 7
Bouvier, John Vernou IV (cousin once
removed), 98
Bouvier, John Vernou Jr. "Grampy
Jack" (grandfather)
background of, 3, 9
compiles family history, 34–37
death of, 109, 111–112
diary of, 19–20, 137
and family fortune, 111–112, 138,
173
Bouvier, John Vernou Sr. (great-
grandfather), 2, 9, 23
Bouvier, Louise Vernou (great-great-
grandmother), 11, 35, 37–38, 137
Bouvier, Maude. *See* Davis, Maude
Bouvier (aunt)
Bouvier, Maude Sergeant
(grandmother), 3, 5, 51
Bouvier, Michel "Big Boy" (cousin),
17, 21, 39, 55, 93, 98, 112
Bouvier, Michel Charles "M.C." (great-
great-uncle), 19, 20, 21
background of, 2–3
and family fortune, 19, 20, 21,
111–112, 172

Bouvier, Michel Charles "M.C."
(*continued*)
New York brownstone of, 33, 38
papers of, 137
Bouvier, Michel (great-great-
grandfather), 1–2, 11, 35, 37,
38–39
Bouvier, Michel IV (cousin once
removed), 98
Bouvier, William Sergeant "Bud"
(uncle), 3, 7, 17
Bouvier family
decline of family fortune, 111–112,
138, 173
in society, 21, 23, 178
view of Kennedy family, 178
Bowdin, Helen, 114
Bowdin, Judy, 114, 116
Bowdoin, Aileen, 173
Buckingham Palace, 116
Butler, Sally, 115–116

Camelot Gardens, 178
Canfield, Cass, 164
Canfield, Michael, 164, 168–169, 185
Cassini, Igor. *See* Knickerbocker,
Cholly
Cavanagh, John, 189
Charapovitsky, Maya, 82
Churchill, Winston, 117, 166
Curtis, Charlotte, 121
Cushing, Richard, 189, 190

Danseuse (horse), 74, 96, 98, 100, 102,
158
Davis, John E. (uncle), 8, 189, 190, 191,
192, 193
Davis, John H. (cousin)
birth of, 17
earliest recollection of JB, 21
at Hammersmith Farm, 125–128
lunch with JB in Washington,
161–163
meets John F. Kennedy, 167–168
in Navy, 157–158, 159–160
and sale of Lasata, 136–137

Davis, Maude Bouvier (aunt), 61, 79,
95
birth of, 5
and family fortune, 112
and JB's wedding, 186, 189–190,
191, 192–193, 194
marries John E. Davis, 8
Debutante of the Year, 107–109, 168
Delacorte Press, 155
de Mohrenschildt, George, 63, 75, 92
de Rossiére, Harriet, 120
Devon Yacht Club, 46–47, 50, 55
Drexel, Emma Bouvier (great-great-
aunt), 38

East Hampton, Long Island. *See*
Bouvier, Jacqueline Lee,
summers in East Hampton
Ehret, Louis, 166
Eisenhower, Dwight D., 160–161
Eisenhower, Mamie, 174
Elizabeth II (queen of England),
coronation of, 173
Ewing, Caroline. *See* Bouvier, Caroline
Ewing (great-grandmother)

Farrington, Kip, 98
Fay, Red, 172, 183
Ferguson, Joan Ellis, 120
Foley, Edward F., 114, 116
Friede, Eleanor, 155

Gardiner, Robert Lion, 47
George VI (king of England), 117
George Washington University, 139,
141, 142, 152
Gore, T. B., 82
Gracie Square (New York home),
64–65, 75
Grampy Jack. *See* Bouvier, John
Vernou Jr. "Grampy Jack"
(grandfather)
Grey Gardens (East Hampton home), 8,
44, 136, 163
Grosvenor, Rose, 102
Guyot de Renty, Countess, 132–133

Hammersmith Farm
  background of, 80, 82
  and Danseuse, 98, 100
  impression of, 173
  JB at, 84, 100, 102
  and JB's wedding, 190, 191, 193
  John H. Davis at, 125–126, 128
  sale of, 178
Harper & Row, 164
Harper's Bazaar, 168, 169
Herter, Albert, 10, 12, 13
Heymann, David, 166
Hiroshima, 98
Holton-Arms (school), 85, 114
Hufty, Page, 136
Husted, John G. W., 114, 159

Jennings, Emma Brewster, 82
Jennings, Oliver B., 82

Keller, James, 189
Kennedy, Joan, 183
Kennedy, John F.
  becomes engaged to JB, 176
  described, 159, 167, 172
  elected to U.S. Senate, 160–161
  father's ambition for, 171, 177
  and JB's spending habits, 122
  meets Jack Bouvier, 164, 166–167
  meets JB, 159
  meets John H. Davis, 167–168
  prenuptial events, 184, 185, 186–187
  relationship with JB, 138, 158,
    160–168, 170, 171–174, 176, 177
  on wedding day, 191–192
Kennedy, Joseph P. Jr., 170
Kennedy, Joseph P. Sr.
  Bouvier family view of, 166, 178
  friendship with Arthur Krock, 158
  James T. Lee's view of, 179
  and JB's prenuptial events, 184, 185,
    186, 187
  relationship with JB, 170, 171–173
  view of son's marriage to JB, 177
  and wedding of JB and John F.
    Kennedy, 188–189, 190, 191

Kennedy, Kathleen, 158, 170
Kennedy family, 170–172, 177, 178
Kimmerle, Bertha, 49–50, 52, 56,
    57–58, 63–64
Knickerbocker, Cholly, 107–109, 168
Krock, Arthur, 158

Lasata (East Hampton home). *See also*
    Bouvier, Jacqueline Lee,
    summers in East Hampton
  after death of Grampy Jack, 114
  description of, 8–14
  grounds of, 12–14, 92–93
  sale of, 114, 130, 136–138
Lazy "A" Bar Ranch, 73
Lee, James T. (grandfather)
  background of, 23–24
  in East Hampton, 46, 113
  family of, 50–51, 53, 54
  relationship with Jack Bouvier, 20,
    64, 65, 66
  view of JB's marriage to John F.
    Kennedy, 179
Lee, Janet. *See* Auchincloss, Janet Lee
    (mother)
Lee, Margaret Merritt (grandmother),
    50, 54
Lincoln, Evelyn, 180
Little Edie. *See* Beale, Edith "Little
    Edie" (cousin)
Lodge, Henry Cabot, 160, 163, 171
Louis Phillipe (king of France), 12, 33
Louis XVIII (king of France), 1
Lowell, Florence, 114

Macdonald, Torbert, 183
Maidstone Club, 46, 55, 57, 76, 92,
    95
Marga Maude. *See* Bouvier, Maude
    Sergeant (grandmother)
Mayflower Hotel, 161
Merritt, Margaret A.. *See* Lee, Margaret
    Merritt
Merrywood (Virginia home), 80, 82,
    85, 87, 141–142, 158, 169, 170,
    173

Mesta, Perle, 161, 173
Miss Chapin's School, 28, 30, 52, 58, 71, 76
Miss Porter's School, 95–96, 100–102

Newey, Bertha, 51
New York Times, 158
Norton, Sue, 96

Obolensky, Prince Serge, 92
O'Brien, Larry, 172, 183
O'Donnell, Kenney, 172
Olmstead, Frederick Law, 125
Onassis, Aristotle, 8, 39, 47, 92, 122–123, 155
One Special Summer, 27, 95, 96, 152–155
Oswald, Lee Harvey, 63
Our Forebears, 34–37, 132

Perelman, Ron, 9
Peters, Ralph, 128
Plugge, Anne, 76, 85, 87, 95, 133–134
Point Breeze (home), 1
Powers, Dave, 172, 183
Prix de Paris competition. *See Vogue* magazine Prix de Paris competition
Putnam, Harrington, 189, 190, 191, 192, 193

Queen Elizabeth (ship), 152
Queen Mary (ship), 116

Radziwill, Lee. *See* Bouvier, Caroline "Lee" (sister)
Roosevelt, Franklin D., 3, 97–98, 166
Ross, Joan Kupfer, 121
Rossiter, Francis, 189
Rutherford, Lewis, 97

Sandison, Helen, 114
Sarah Lawrence College, 154, 157, 168
Scott, Don, 128

Scott, Henry C. Scott Jr. "Scotty" (cousin), 17, 39, 61
Scott, Henry C. (uncle), 8
Scott, Michelle Bouvier (aunt), 61, 63, 79, 95, 111
    birth of, 5
    and family fortune, 112
    and JB's wedding, 186, 189–191, 192–193, 194
    marries Henry C. Scott, 8
Scott, Shella (cousin), 17, 96
Securities and Exchange Commission, 166
Sergeant, Maude. *See* Bouvier, Maude Sergeant (grandmother)
Shearman, Helen, 114
Social Register, 21
Sorbonne, 119, 133, 135
Standard Oil Co., 82, 125
stock market crash, 17, 19–20
Stringfellow, Ethel, 30, 52, 76

Thayer, Mary Van Rensselaer, 131
Tuckerman, Nancy, 96
Turnure, Pamela, 182

Vassar College, 107, 119–121, 124
Vernou, John (ancestor), 38
Vernou, Louise. *See* Bouvier, Louise Vernou (great-great-grandmother)
Vidal, Gore, 82, 84, 87
Vidal, Nina Gore, 82, 84
Vogue magazine Prix de Paris competition, 142–144, 146–151
Vreeland, Diana, 168

Waldrop, Frank, 158
Walsh, Thomas, 177
Washington Times-Herald, JB's job at, 158–159, 160, 161, 162, 163, 173, 174
Wildmoor (East Hampton home), 25, 43, 130, 137